An Introduction to
Environmental
Archaeology

P.1.89
P
26/3

An Introduction to

Environmental Archaeology

John G. Evans

Senior Lecturer in Archaeology, University College, Cardiff

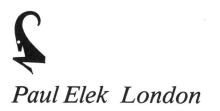

Paul Elek London

First published in Great Britain in 1978 by
Elek Books Ltd
54-58 Caledonian Road, London N1 9RN

©John G. Evans 1978

ISBN 0 236 40110 6 (cased)
ISBN 0 236 40111 4 (paper)

Printed in Great Britain by Unwin Brothers Ltd.
The Gresham Press, Woking, Surrey

For
Dickon, Ailinor and Thomas

Contents

Figures

Preface

Environmental archaeology is the study of the past environment of man. This book is intended as a simple introduction to theoretical aspects of the subject, and has been written specifically for first and second year university students reading archaeology and related subjects such as environmental studies. It is also intended for extra-mural students, and for both professional and part-time arch-aeologists, particularly those engaged in their own excavations. But the book is in no way intended as a field manual or practical hand-book.

The book falls logically into three sections. Chapter 1 comprises a short introduction to the various factors of the human environ-ment. Chapters 2, 3 and 4 look at the main techniques and evidence — plants, animals, soils and sediments — used in the recon-struction of past environments. And Chapters 5 and 6 examine some of the more common environmental situations — such as caves, coastlines and archaeological monuments — to which these techniques and evidence can be applied.

It has not been possible, or even desirable, to discuss the evidence *for* all the environmental factors since this would involve undue repetition. For example, the multiple nature of the evidence for ancient vegetation is implicit in the various sections of Chapter 2 on plant remains, although fauna and soils may also be used as a guide. Where problems do arise — and climate is a case in point — the diverse classes of evidence are mentioned under the relevant headings in Chapter 1.

For ease of reference, an outline of the main stages of the Pleistocene and the associated archaeological periods is presented as a series of tables (Tables 3 to 6) in an appendix (p.130). There is also a glossary of terms not formally explained in the text (p.135). No previous knowledge in the reader of either scientific subjects or archaeology is assumed.

I would like to thank Professor G. W. Dimbleby for reading the first draft of this book and for making a number of valuable com-ments. All the line drawings are the painstaking work of Howard Mason who has my warmest thanks.

J. G. Evans
Cardiff, May 1977

1 The human environment

As an introduction to environmental archaeology this book describes the various techniques and indicators used in working out the environment of ancient human communities, and the various situations in which these techniques and indicators may be applied. Interpretation of the evidence is not always easy, and considerable attention must therefore be paid to this aspect, especially in the case of the more controversial indicators like insects. It is important at every stage for the student to bear in mind the origin or source of the evidence, how it came to be in its present state and position of preservation, and upon precisely what aspect of the environment it bears. The distinctions between climatic and local environmental indicators, and between evidence of a far-travelled and of a local nature are particularly important to grasp. All this is especially crucial in dealing with *human* environments where the effects of climate and local environment are often difficult to separate from those of human activities.

As mentioned in the Preface this book is not a practical laboratory or field manual. Neither is it an account of environmental history — as presented in an earlier work (Evans, 1975) — nor an account of the various inter-reactions of man and environment ('man/land relationships') as dealt with by Butzer (1972) and Cornwall (1964). The student must be clear about these various distinctions so that he can appreciate precisely what he is reading about, and precisely where, in the broader study of human environment, this book fits.

However, before describing the various forms of evidence — which is done in Chapters 2 to 6 — it is necessary in this introductory chapter to outline and discuss briefly the main factors of man's environment.

Environmental factors

The human environment includes every conceivable factor of man's surroundings, from the earth's magnetic field to the smallest virus, which might affect his mode of life or to which he might adapt. In practice, however, and as far as the environmental

archaeologist is concerned, there is a set of fairly well-defined para-
meters into which the environment can be broken down and for
which there is evidence in the fossil record. These can be listed as
follows:

Climate
    Precipitation — rain and snow
    Temperature
    Seasonality
    Wind and exposure
    Length of growing season
Geology
    Distribution of major land masses
    Distribution of major volcanic and earthquake zones
    Land forms — topography
    Inorganic raw materials — minerals and rocks
Soil
Vegetation
    Part exploited for food
    Part exploited for other purposes
    Habitat
Fauna
    Part exploited for food
    Part exploited for other purposes
    Habitat
Diseases

Less obvious, but equally important, factors are the elements of
spatial and *temporal variability* — space and time.

The impact of *man* himself on the environment, and the several
repercussions of this impact for the environment and the human
species, although last mentioned, are without doubt among the
most critical factors. There are arguments for and against treating
man as a distinct species, separate from other animals; these are
briefly discussed at the end of this chapter.

A precise hierarchical classification of all these environmental
factors is impossible, and there are many interactions. Four useful,
although somewhat artificial, groups to bear in mind are the
following:

(1) Parts of the environment exploited by man for food.
(2) Parts of the environment exploited by man for other pur-
     poses; e.g. timber, hides, inorganic raw materials.
(3) Parts of the environment not always directly exploited by

man but affecting him; e.g. climate, vegetation, disease.

(4) Parts of the environment not always exploited by or affecting man, but which are useful in working out the ancient environment.

Climate (Lamb, 1972; Manley, 1962; Raikes, 1967)

Climate is the primary environmental control affecting man both directly, and indirectly through its influence on other factors such as fauna, vegetation and soil. Climate determines which parts of the earth's surface are suitable for the cultivation of crops. The nature of the climax vegetation — tundra, steppe or forest — is determined by climate; so too is the associated mammalian fauna (but see p.39). This is fundamental to hunting communities in determining their life-style. Clothing and house type also come under the influence of climate.

Climate can be broken down into *precipitation* — rain and snow — and *temperature*. A combination of these factors is relevant to the initiation, growth and decay of ice sheets. These control major changes in the distribution of land and sea which in turn control local aspects of climate.

The evidence for past climates is diverse and presents many problems of interpretation, problems highlighted by Raikes (1967). One of the main difficulties is in distinguishing between the effects of precipitation and the effects of other factors. Large thicknesses of flood deposits may accumulate in a very short time due to freak weather conditions, tectonic disturbance (earth movements) or human interference with the land surface — e.g. forest clearance and tillage. Evidence for rainfall comes from situations such as peat bogs or infilled lakes where differences in rate of peat growth or lake level may be interpreted in climatic terms. Soils, or land surfaces, within these deposits indicate periods of dryness. Wind-blown deposits are also indicative of dry climates with interstratified soils reflecting damper conditions. But the influence of vegetational changes is hard to assess.

The presence of chianophilous — or snow-loving — plants is indicative of considerable snow-cover for part of the year.

Temperature and rainfall are closely linked. A rise of temperature will lead to an increase in evaporation from the soil surface and thus to drier conditions without attendant rainfall change. It is perhaps more useful to think in terms of the precipitation/evaporation ratio rather than rainfall *per se*.

Evidence for former temperatures is largely biological and rests on the distribution of various plant and animal species (Fig.19).

The present distribution of many plants and animals is controlled by temperature or other climatic factors acting either singly or together. If, therefore, the remains of a particular species are found outside its present range, one can infer a change in that area of the controlling factor. Species whose distribution is fairly precisely controlled by a single climatic parameter and which occur frequently and widely in ancient soils and sediments are known as *indicator species*. The main problem is that we depend largely on present-day ranges of the various organisms and these may be controlled by factors other than climate. The distribution of many of the large wild mammals, for example, is mainly determined by man. Smaller creatures, in particular the insects, are more reliable although even these may not occupy their full potential climatic range due to the presence of unsuitable habitats. Past distributions, too, may be determined by factors other than climate. Ideally we need to use species whose physiological tolerance of a range of temperatures and humidities has been established by laboratory experiment. In practice this has seldom been done. We know largely by inference that some of the most reliable groups are various species of plant, the small mammals, insects and Foraminifera.

Species diversity (p.7) can also be used as a guide.

Other methods of working out palaeotemperatures are oxygen isotope analysis (p.62), applicable mainly to marine sediments, and dendrochronology (p.28), of more value in the study of terrestrial sites.

Different sediments and soils have also been used. Screes for example are generally indicative of periglacial conditions, travertine of milder climates (p.70). There are problems in making inferences from cave deposits which form in environments less extreme than that of the general ambience. Soils have been much used in the study of Pleistocene climates in Europe and North America to indicate the status of warm periods, particularly whether interstadial or interglacial. On the whole, less mature soils of high base status form during interstadials, more mature soils showing greater or lesser signs of leaching — the removal of minerals and other nutrients by downwashing (p.73) — during interglacials.

Seasonality of climate is concerned with climatic variation throughout the year. In Ice Age Europe seasonal differences were less marked than they are today in Arctic regions, with warmer summers and milder winters, due to the lower latitude and more uniform day length. The climate of periglacial Europe finds no present-day parallels and this is reflected in unfamiliar combinations of fauna and vegetation. In Mediterranean countries, seasonality of rainfall, with warm dry summers and wet winters with sudden and very heavy rain storms, is an important factor in causing soil erosion. Massive thicknesses of hillwash build up in valleys.

Soil type — in particular the movement of various compounds of iron — is also a guide to seasonality. But human interference with the forest vegetation exposes the land surface to greater extremes and in temperate regions may lead to the development of features more characteristic of strongly seasonal climates (p.78). The continental climate with hot, dry summers and cold, dry winters is characterized by chernozems (p.78).

The length of the growing season and aspects of *weather* such as wind and exposure are relevant to the growth and ripening of crops and the precise positioning of settlements.

Geology (Pitty, 1971; Sparks, 1971)

The gross distribution of continents and oceans has provided the main stage on which the evolution of man and the development and history of the various human races has been played. The isolation of Australia and the difficulties of access to the New World via the Bering Strait land bridge were important factors in the late spread of human groups to these continents and their subsequent isolation.

Geology and landforms are the media through which climate operates. On a local scale, topography — especially in areas of marked altitudinal contrast — is important. Mountain ranges develop climatic contrasts which in areas of uniform terrain are a function of latitude. Aspects of Ice Age life may there find echo in microcosmic form.

This is especially relevant to the phenomenon of transhumance. In many parts of the world — western and northern Britain, Scandinavia, Spain, Greece and the Zagros Mountains of Iran — the long-distance movement of flocks and herds by farming peoples takes place twice a year. This is a strategy for exploiting the environment where there are strong seasonal contrasts in herbaceous plant growth. In winter, animals are kept close to the settlement and fed on fodder collected during the previous summer. In spring the animals are taken to upland pasture and kept there through to the early autumn. The phenomenon is also a natural feature of animal populations — long migrations often taking place, to which the seasonal activities of human hunting groups may sometimes have been adjusted.

Mountain ranges, coastlines, lakes and river valleys are of importance in providing variability in the environment and are often the determining factor in the positioning of ecotones — the boundary zones between two major environmental systems (p.9). They are also of significance in controlling routeways and communications.

Rocks and minerals of various kinds were exploited by early man for building materials, tools and weapons (Rosenfeld, 1965). Generally exploitation was on a local basis — the geology of an area is often reflected in its building — but in some cases, particularly for tools and weapons, exploitation went further afield. In Britain, various igneous rocks in the west were exploited in Neolithic and Bronze Age times for the manufacture of axes, and were trafficked widely, often occurring hundreds of kilometres from source (Shotton, 1968). Another rock widely utilized and moved over long distances in antiquity was the black volcanic glass, obsidian (Dixon, *et al.*, 1968). This was used for knives, daggers, and other artefacts such as sickles for which an extremely sharp cutting edge was vital; it was also used for mirrors, one of the earliest examples being from the Neolithic town of Çatal Hüyük in Anatolia (Mellaart, 1967).

The movement of raw materials on a wide scale opened up all kinds of possibilities for cultural contact, the exchange of goods and ideas, and the exploitation of new environments which may not otherwise have been realized.

Soil (Cornwall, 1958; Limbrey, 1975)

Soil type appears to have controlled — either directly, or indirectly through its influence on vegetation — the distribution of various cultures and human groups on both a large and a small scale. The precise way in which this factor operates is, however, still unclear in most cases. A few examples may be mentioned. The hunter–gatherer communities of later Mesolithic Britain and Europe favoured areas of light sandy soil, areas which are now often heath or moorland (Tringham, 1971). Heavier soils and those of the calcareous loess lands (p.78) were largely — although not entirely — ignored. One possible reason for this is that the woody vegetation of the lighter, less nutrient-rich soils favoured by Mesolithic man was more easily fired and replaced by grassland — or sometimes heath — which, as discussed later (p.11), is a prime requisite for human hunting communities.

Early prehistoric farmers, on the other hand, tended to settle the calcareous soils of loess and limestone, although again not exclusively (Clark, 1952). In this case it is felt that ease of tillage and high fertility were important factors. Heavier loams and clays were not, on the whole, taken in until the development, in historical times, of the mould-board plough — a type of plough capable of turning the soil over.

The relationship between man and soil type is complex. It is bound up with all sorts of factors like drainage, fertility, texture and the vegetation the soil supports, as well as human land-use strategies — which may be in part culturally determined anyway — and with the level of man's technological development.

Plants (Dimbleby, 1967)

Not a lot is known about the plant foods of prehistoric man due to the infrequent preservation of remains, although there is enough to show that a wide variety of species was exploited (Brothwell and Brothwell, 1969). What is difficult to assess is the relative importance of plant to animal foods in man's diet. If the practices of present-day primitive communities can be used as a guide it can be suggested that people living in tropical climates were more dependent on plant foods and exploited a greater range than people inhabiting cold-climate regions. Woodland, too, provides a greater variety than open habitats. It is unlikely, however, that, prior to the development of domesticated plants and their cultivation on a large scale, any prehistoric peoples were dependent solely on plants for food.

Plants have also been exploited for a whole variety of other purposes, particularly timber for the construction of houses and trackways, and the manufacture of tools and weapons. The availability of timber may often have been an important determinant in the architecture of dwellings.

As part of man's environment the plant world impinges in many ways. Most important is the relative abundance of forested to open land — the *structure* of the vegetation rather than its precise species composition (Clark, 1952; 1967). We have already hinted at this in mentioning the exploitation of plants for food. Vegetation structure also controls the structure and species composition of animal populations, and this has considerable repercussions on man's hunting techniques, the range of species hunted, and his life-style. In tundra, there are large herds of a few, gregarious, species such as reindeer. All the vegetation above ground is available to the animals but little of it is directly edible for man. The animals are relatively easy to track and kill. By contrast, in a forested environment not only is part of the land surface taken up by the trunks of the trees themselves but most of the foliage is in the canopy, out of reach of grazing and browsing animals. Consequently there are fewer large herbivores, although a greater range of species (Elton, 1927). They go around in smaller groups and they are often species that are shy and difficult to hunt.

Animals (Chaplin, 1971; Cornwall, 1956, 1968; Kurtén, 1968)

Animals, too, can be divided into those that are directly exploited for food or other purposes, and those that affect man in other ways. The structure of mammal populations needs no further mention at this stage as the subject has just been aired. It must not be forgotten, however, that a large number of creatures lower than the mammals on the evolutionary scale were also exploited for food — birds, reptiles, insects and molluscs (Brothwell and Brothwell, 1969). And the aquatic habitats of lake, river, coast and deep sea provided a welcome — often necessary — alternative to the terrestrial ambience for prehistoric man, as is attested by the many skeletal remains of animals such as seal, salmon, whale and polar bear among the bone debris of ancient sites, and rock engravings from Norway of men engaged in the hunting of killer whale from very flimsy boats.

Animals were also exploited for other purposes — clothing, gut, bone for tools, weapons and fuel, traction and pets (Ucko and Dimbleby, 1969). Ice Age communities used the bones of mammoths as supports for tents which were probably made of the hide of the same animal.

Animals, although perhaps less so than plants, play a part in the habitat of man aside from food and the other uses just mentioned. As transmitters of disease many species are important, some, such as the flea and the mosquito, affecting man directly, others, like the beetle responsible for carrying Dutch elm disease, being of less immediate impact. The large carnivores — e.g. shark, lion and cave bear — have always been a problem, particularly when exploiting the same habitat as man (Fig.14).

For the environmental archaeologist there are also many species of animal and plant that have, on the whole, little interaction with man but that are useful indicators of other, more relevant, aspects of the environment like climate and land-use. In this category we can include, for example, the snails (Evans, 1972). Although some species are eaten by man and others are vectors of human and farm animal parasites, most of those recovered from archaeological and environmental deposits are present as incidental and non-participant members of the human environment. But their value in reconstructing the ancient environment of areas such as the loess plains of central and eastern Europe is very great (Ložek, 1964).

Spatial variability (Ager, 1963)

We have already hinted at the importance of spatial variability in discussing transhumance and in the exploitation of different vegetational types and their animal communities. The animal and plant communities of an area together with the non-living environmental components constitute the *ecosystem* (Odum, 1963), and we can recognize two basic types — specialized and generalized. Specialized ecosystems are those such as tundra, steppe and prairie in which, on the whole, there is little variation or diversity in the animal and plant communities. There are exceptions, such as the African grasslands which have an unusual diversity of mammals. Generalized ecosystems are those such as woodland, particularly in hill country, where a variety of habitats — trees, open areas, lakes and rivers — are closely juxtaposed. Trees introduce a much greater number of niches into an ecosystem than is the case with open habitats, and the number of different species and ecological types is greater also.

The transition zone between two major environments such as forest and plain or aquatic and terrestrial is an area of optimum plant and animal resources in which the ecosystem is at its most diverse. It is known as an *ecotone* (van Waateringe, 1968). Such areas were, and still are, favoured by both man and animals for exploitation and habitation.

Time

The time factor is hard to assess in its importance for early man. Many environmental processes — for example the more long-term climatic changes and the major shifts in forest composition — probably took place too slowly to have a noticeable effect in a single human lifetime. Others were more rapid — for example sea-level changes at the end of the Last Glaciation — and may have had a major impact in a very short time.

The environmental archaeologist is closely concerned with the time factor in that most of the sites he deals with encompass a period of environmental change. Comparison of the life-style of different cultures living in different environments and/or at different periods, and the search for environmental causes for various cultural changes, have been a major preoccupation with prehistorians and geographers. As the late E. S. Higgs (1972) pointed out: 'The typological framework [of prehistory] encouraged the view that successive peoples or tribes played out their lives against the background of nature, and the climatic and vegetational zones of the natural scientist provide a ready-made framework into which stylistic entities could be made to fit.' But Higgs went on to stress various drawbacks in this view, the main one being that: ' . . . the attributes that define a particular climatic or vegetational zone do not necessarily impinge on human activities within it, while, if they do, it does not follow that a change in zonal properties will meet with a corresponding change in response.'

J. G. D. Clark has recently made the same point in a slightly different context. The economy of a community and other aspects of its life-style such as domestic architecture, clothing and settlement pattern have been considered in the past as being controlled by the environment. This approach — known as *environmental determinism* — was formerly popular with geographers, historians and archaeologists. Today its appeal is less strong and there is more of a trend to see man's life-style as being 'adapted to' the environment rather than being 'determined by' it. As Clark (1975) states: 'Economic arrangements made by prehistoric communities were not controlled by but rather were adjusted to available natural resources.'

On the same subject, there are a number of practical problems that arise when attempts are made to equate causally culture and environment. Firstly, factual information — the raw data — on both the archaeological and environmental sides has often not been sufficiently precise to allow for correlation. Secondly, very few workers have the necessary detailed background knowledge about both culture and environment to correlate the two anyway. And thirdly, it is often the case that sites suitable for environmental work have no associated archaeology, and vice versa. Recent workers have begun to tackle this problem. In Southern France, prehistorians excavating at various early Stone Age and Neanderthal cave sites, particularly the cave of l'Hortus (Fig.14), have encompassed the human environment, the cultural debris and the human skeletal material in precise and equal detail (de Lumley, 1972). Too often in the past only one aspect has been tackled. Other areas of similarly intense research include early farming sites in Iran (Hole and Flannery, 1967) and the Neolithic colonization of northern Ireland (Case, 1969). Various town sites both in Britain and on the continent of Europe are also providing a wealth of environmental data in contexts suitably associated with cultural material (Buckland, 1967; Thompson, 1967).

Man (Thomas, 1956; Evans and Limbrey, 1975)

We now know that man himself, even on occasion as far back as the Old Stone Age, was of critical importance in moulding his own environment. Processes such as deforestation, soil erosion and game overkill can be attributed to man well prior to the development of farming. The earliest true axes in the world, dating from the beginning of the second decachiliad, come from Arnhem Land, Australia, a continent which saw no agriculture until the European colonization of the late eighteenth century.

The impact of prehistoric man on the landscape was first recognized in the pollen record during the early 1940s by workers in Denmark and Britain (Iversen, 1941; Godwin, 1944). Farming communities were seen to have cleared off the forest vegetation in order to grow cereal crops and open up land for sheep grazing. More recently it has been shown that earlier hunter–gatherer peoples were also responsible for attacking the environment, and during the last ten years or so there has been a number of papers demonstrating various aspects of this attack (Smith, 1970).

But how far should we consider these instances to be unique to man?

A major problem is that the investigation of forest history has taken place against a background of the concept of the vegetation *climatic climax* (e.g. Tansley, 1939). Each climatic region of the world is said to have its own climax vegetation which is reached through a succession of stages — known as a *sere* — if not deflected or interfered with by man. Over most of the British Isles this is mixed deciduous woodland. Other climatic climaxes are tundra, the north European conifer belt and the Mediterranean evergreen forest. But climax vegetations are less uniform than is often realized, and this is due in large measure to the animal communities within them. Animals are now seen to be of much greater import in determining the structure and composition of the natural vegetation than was appreciated in the early decades of this century when the concept of the climatic climax was first formulated. The larger herbivores, for example, cannot on the whole survive in closed woodland without some open ground on which to feed during the winter months. Clearings, particularly around springs and river banks, once formed, are easily enlarged by overgrazing, and the rich herbaceous vegetation that springs up attracts even greater numbers of animals. Furthermore, there have been a number of major shifts of climate and changes of soil type in the past, which has tended to disrupt the forest vegetation. Taking these factors into account, the concept of a long-established and stable climax vegetation becomes less sound.

If we accept, therefore, that the forest vegetation is not a uniform 'all pervasive' cover but contains within it refugia of open ground and patches of sub-climax vegetation which change in their area and distribution through time, we need not view man's part in controlling the landscape as being in any way very different from that of the animals. He may be considered as an additional animal in the ecosystem attracted to the same habitats and for the same reasons, but he should not be selected out as a creature of unique importance.

The story as far as man's impact on animal populations is concerned is, interestingly, more or less precisely the reverse. Stone Age hunters were formerly considered to hunt and kill their prey in a straightforward aggressive predator/prey relationship. However, following a suggestion of J. G. D. Clark (1952) that Upper Palaeolithic man may have herded reindeer and lived in some sort of loose symbiotic, or mutually advantageous, relationship with the herds, there has been much recent work on the possibilities of pre-Neolithic management or semi-domestication of various animals (Jarman, 1972). There are plenty of examples of this sort of relationship *within* the animal kingdom (Zeuner, 1963). Again, therefore, the position of man within the ecosystem is seen as being somewhat less than unique.

The situation today is different. Man has survived, and even benefited in the past from adverse physical environmental conditions. Indeed, there is really no such thing as a good or a bad environment, only the familiar and the unfamiliar. Man is often stimulated by the unfamiliar to closer, more interlocking, adaptations with the environment. However, this does not mean that we should condone the damage being done by man to the environment today. 'What man has not before had to face is the threat to the life-support systems which is so evident today' (Dimbleby, 1976). In this respect, at least, the human population is unique.

2 Plant remains

Before describing the various types of biological material that may be used in environmental reconstruction, a number of general points must be made. The basic principle in utilizing plants and animals is that each species lives in a particular habitat which may be more or less clearly defined. With reference to their present-day habitat preferences and geographical ranges, remains of organisms in ancient deposits can be used to reconstruct former environments. But there are two major groups of problems. The first concerns the way in which the structure and composition of living populations becomes distorted at death by various depositional and destructional processes (Ager, 1963). The second is concerned with ecological aspects of the organisms themselves (West, 1968).

In the first group we can recognize three stages (Fig.1):

(1) The living population of animals and plants.
(2) The death assemblage.
(3) The fossil or subfossil assemblage.

The death assemblage is the grouping of organisms at death before any depositional or destructional processes occur. Gravity brings

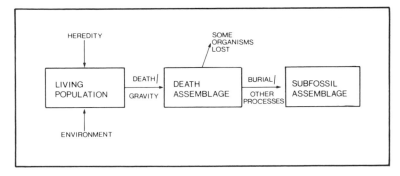

Fig.1. Stages in the formation of a subfossil assemblage.

all organisms that live at or above the ground into a single layer on the ground surface. In effect, what was once a three-dimensional arrangement of species becomes a two-dimensional one. Organisms living high in the forest canopy or on a cliff face become associated with the remains of ground-living species.

Subsequently, various other processes — differential destruction, soil erosion, stream action and so on — alter the death assemblage to the extent that not only may it be deposited with death assemblages from other environments, but only part of the death assemblage will remain. For example, in acid soils, bone and shell will be destroyed, but pollen will remain. River deposits may contain marsh and terrestrial organisms as well as those once living in the river. Interpretation must therefore take these processes into account.

In the second group there are two somewhat unrelated points to be made. First, some plants and animals changed their habitat preferences during the past. Others have become extinct. We can, therefore, only interpret their ecology in terms of associated species and other, non-biological, indicators of the environment. Further, present-day geographical ranges may not be altogether climatically controlled; other factors, especially man, may be involved. We must, therefore, beware of using only one species in environmental reconstruction. Whole populations should be employed.

The second point concerns what is probably the most long-standing problem in palaeoecology. To what extent does an animal or plant species found in a subfossil assemblage reflect the environment as a whole? This is of particular importance on archaeological sites where the influence of local, man-made, habitats is often considerable, masking the effects of regional environment and climate (Fig.7). In environmental reconstruction we must always take into account the *regional* and *local* aspects. Different groups of organisms, different species and different environmental situations will yield information weighed in favour of one or the other. For example, pollen, particularly from peat bogs and lake sediments (Fig.6), will on the whole yield information about regional vegetational history; pollen from soils is usually of more local origin. Insects are better indicators of climate than snails or plants, since they react faster to changes.

These and other problems, particularly the various effects of man, will be further considered in this and the following chapter.

Pollen analysis (Dimbleby, 1967; Faegri and Iversen, 1964; Godwin, 1956)

The pollen grains of plants are preserved in anaerobic and acid deposits and soils (Fig.2). They can be extracted, identified under

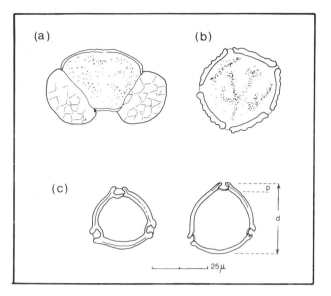

Fig.2. Pollen grains. (a) Pine. (b) Elm. (c) Tree birch (*Betula pubescens*) (left) and dwarf birch (*Betula nana*) (right) to show the method of distinguishing between two similar pollen types, in this case by measuring the ratio of grain diameter (d) to pore depth (p). (From Walker, 1955)

the microscope, and counted. The relative abundance of the various groups present can be used to reconstruct former vegetation. This technique is known as pollen analysis. It is probably the most widely used technique of environmental archaeology and certainly the one with most popular appeal.

Samples for analysis are taken either by various coring techniques or from open sections. Extraction and concentration of the pollen is greatly aided by the fact that the outer coat or *exine* of the grain is extremely resistant to chemical attack. For example, if a sample of soil containing pollen is placed in a glass beaker and treated with hydrofluoric acid the soil will be destroyed — so will the beaker! — and only the pollen will remain. Special containers are obviously necessary for this sort of treatment. Once extracted, the pollen can be concentrated by centrifugation, stained to make it more visible, and examined under the microscope.

The results of pollen analysis are best presented in histogram form as a *pollen diagram* (Fig.3). This is simply a graph in which the vertical axis is the soil or sediment column with the depth below

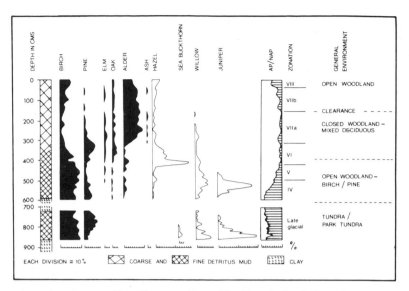

Fig.3. Specimen pollen diagram. Tree (black) and shrub (open) curves through Late-Devensian and Flandrian lake sediments in Nant Ffrancon, North Wales. The curves shown black (AP) make up the total on which all the percentages are calculated. The ratio AP/NAP shows the changing porportions of arboreal pollen (forest) and non-arboreal pollen (other vegetation). (From Seddon, 1962)

surface (or a convenient datum) indicated at intervals, and the horizontal axis the relative abundance of the various species or groups of pollen grain. In the vertical axis, symbols are used to depict the different sediment types. Along the horizontal axis, the methods of working out and depicting relative abundance vary. Often each group is represented as a percentage of total tree pollen, in which case the histograms for the tree species are indicated in a manner different from those of the shrubs and herbs. In other cases, total pollen may be used as a basis for the calculations. Various techniques are used to emphasize specific features — for example different symbols, or differences in horizontal scale. Some pollen diagrams look alarmingly complex at first sight, but most are easy to sort out with patience. On the extreme right of a pollen diagram there is usually a summary interpretation of the environmental changes recorded by the pollen sequence, and an indication of the zonation. The latter may be a local scheme or the basic scheme for the relevant section of the glacial/interglacial system involved.

Another graphical way of presenting the results of pollen

analysis is the *sector diagram* (Fig.4). In this, each species or group is represented as a segment of a circle with a different symbol for each; the total circle is equivalent to 100 per cent. This method can

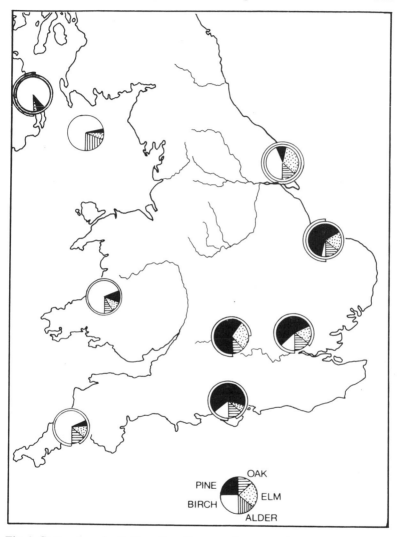

Fig.4. Sector (or pie-dish) pollen diagrams for part of the Boreal period in southern Britain. The hazel is calculated as a percentage over and above the other trees and represented as rings around the main diagrams. Note the differences between the south east and the rest of the area. (From Godwin, 1956)

be used for only one pollen spectrum from any one site, but is a good way of indicating regional differences at any particular time.

Pollen analysis has two main uses which must not be confused. These are *dating* and the *reconstruction of former vegetation*. It is as a dating technique that pollen analysis was first developed and used in an archaeological context. The method was first applied on a large scale to the peat bogs of Denmark, Scandinavia and Britain, and it was shown that the arboreal vegetation over the past 10,000 years consisted of several well-marked zones which reflected changes in forest composition (Godwin, 1956). In addition to the relative abundance of the different tree species, the ratio of tree pollen to non-tree pollen — the TP:NTP (or AP:NAP) ratio (Fig.3) — was used to characterize the zones more closely, and enabled the zonation scheme to be pushed back 4,000 years into the closing stages of the Ice Age (Table 5, p.133). The basis of these major vegetational changes was considered to be climatically controlled and thus the zones were considered synchronous over a wide area. An archaeological find in a peat bog could be dated by analysis of the associated peat and with reference to the standard scheme. This application of pollen analysis to the Late-Devensian and Flandrian periods persisted into the 1960s when it was superseded by radiocarbon dating. It is still used in the study of interglacial deposits.

Of course, as well as being a dating technique, pollen analysis enabled the forest history of a region to be reconstructed. On the whole, however, only the major tree species were counted. Herbaceous and shrub pollen was considered only in so far as it gave a generalized count for the two groups; little attempt was made at subdivision into species.

Early interpretation of Flandrian pollen diagrams had invoked climate as the major controlling factor. Three main zones were recognized (Fig.20; Table 5):

(1) An early zone of climatic amelioration.
(2) A zone of thermal maximum (the 'climatic optimum').
(3) A zone of climatic deterioration.

The last zone was characterized by an increase in the pollen of birch, hornbeam and herbs, and a decline in the pollen of elm — the 'elm decline' — features which were at first interpreted in climatic terms. In the early 1940s, however, two papers were published — one in Britain (Godwin, 1944) and one in Denmark (Iversen, 1941) — demonstrating that the vegetation changes of the later Flandrian were of anthropogenic origin. The elm decline and the appearance of herbaceous species after the mid-Flandrian forest phase were practically synchronous events, and they coincided too with the introduction into the pollen record of various species that are 'weeds of cultivation' — notably plantain, *Plantago* — and, in rare cases, of cereals also. These events were interpreted as reflecting forest clearance and the cultipation of cereals.

In Denmark the record of change was particularly clear, and a number of phases was recognized:

(1) Clearance of woodland, accompanied by the presence of charcoal in the bog stratigraphy.
(2) Cultivation of cereals.
(3) Abandonment, leading to an increase of *Plantago* and bracken.
(4) Regeneration of woodland via a birch phase.

This pattern of temporary clearance is called a 'landnam' — a Danish word meaning literally 'land take' — and has subsequently been widely recognized as a manifestation of the activities of early farming communities in western Europe. The birch is of particular significance in being a species which rapidly colonizes areas cleared by fire.

With the acceptance of the fact that man's activities could be detected in the pollen record, pollen analysis has assumed a whole new purpose. More attention is now paid to the identification of pollen in an attempt to determine species, particularly the herbaceous plants. Where the only difference between two species is in the size of the grain, accurate measurements are made; this applies, for example, to the distinction between such pairs as dwarf birch/tree birch (Fig.2), cereals/grasses and even different species of cereal. The use of scanning electron microscopy enables additional features of pollen grains to be used in identification (Pilcher, 1968). Samples for pollen analysis are taken at closer intervals — down to 0·5 cm (Turner, 1965) — and in the last fifteen years, radiocarbon dating has enabled a fairly precise time scale to be placed on the pollen record. This, for example, has shown that many of the early Neolithic clearances formerly thought to have been of short duration in fact lasted many centuries. They may not, however, reflect the activities of single groups but may be composite clearances reflecting several successive attacks on the different areas of vegetation contributing to the pollen catchment.

As a result of these advances in technique, pollen analysis has become one of the most valuable tools for working out the land-use strategies of prehistoric man.

When first discovered, pollen analysis was applied to peat bogs, particularly where peat cutting had exposed sections through various layers (Fig.46). Later, various coring devices were developed to enable the sampling not only of infilled meres and uncut peat bogs but also of the bottom deposits of large lakes such as those in the English Lake District. From this last area we have a remarkably complete record of environmental change covering the Late-Devensian and Flandrian periods, and including the activities of various human groups (Pennington, 1970; 1975).

Pollen is preserved in both lake sediments and peat by virtue of the anaerobic conditions. Microbial decomposition does not take place. More recently, aerobic acid soils on heath and moorland have been investigated, and these too have yielded high pollen

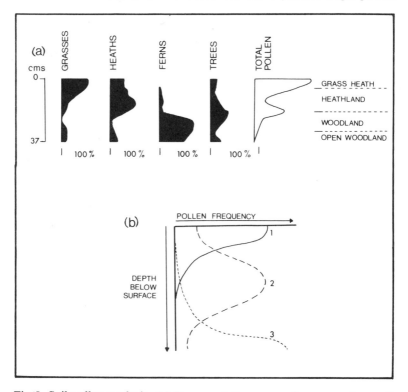

Fig.5. Soil pollen analysis. (a) Representative curves from a modern soil on the uplands of the South Wales coalfield. (From Crampton and Webley, 1964). (b) Diagram showing the distribution of pollen of different ages in a mineral soil. 1, recent pollen; 2, pollen of intermediate age; 3, ancient pollen. (From Evans, 1975)

counts (Dimbleby, 1961). Neutral and calcareous soils are not so suitable and have been little studied (Dimbleby and Evans, 1974). The pollen analysis of soils poses different problems from that of peat and lake sediments. In the latter group the pollen is trapped as it accumulates and there is no further-movement — the pollen is practically contemporary with the sediments. But in the case of soils, the pollen grains move down through the profile, so that not only is the pollen younger than the layers in which it occurs, but there may be mixing of pollen of various ages as well (Fig.5). Nevertheless, as long as these problems are appreciated, valuable results can be, and have been, obtained. In Britain most work has been done on the heathland soils of south-east England and certain upland areas such as Dartmoor and the North York Moors (Dimbleby, 1962).

Another important difference between the pollen analysis of peat bogs and soils is in the origin of the pollen. In the interpretation of pollen diagrams one of the main aims is the separation of local and regional pollen (Tauber, 1967). On the whole, tree pollen tends to travel further than herbaceous pollen. This is most clear in a peat bog or lake where most tree pollen is from the area around the bog/lake (regional), while most of the pollen of mosses, sedges and aquatic plants is from the bog itself (local) (Fig.6). Terrestrial soils,

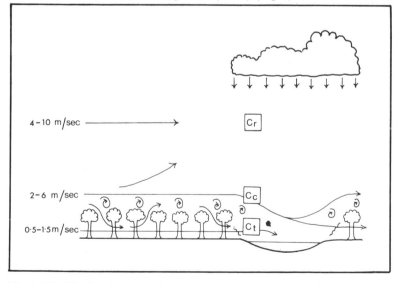

Fig.6. Model of pollen transfer in a forested area. The pollen is transported by three routes: C_t, through the trunk space; C_c, above the canopy; C_r, brought down by rain. (From Tauber, 1967)

on the other hand, generally contain more local herbaceous pollen of plant species relevant to problems of prehistoric land-use. Cereal grains, for example, while often occurring in buried soils, are rarely recovered from peat bogs.

In spite of the difficulties of analysing neutral and calcareous soils and sediments, some successful results have been achieved, particularly from caves. A long and fairly complete sequence spanning the middle part of the Last Glaciation has been obtained from the l'Hortus cave in south-east France (de Lumley, 1972) (Fig.14). However, special techniques of extraction and concentrating the pollen are necessary and, in view of the strong possibility of the differential preservation of certain grains and the destruction of others, interpretation must be done with caution.

Other advances of recent years are the construction of *absolute* pollen diagrams in which the actual pollen rain rather than the abundance of each group relative to the others is plotted (Bonny, 1972), and the construction of *three-dimensional* diagrams (Turner, 1975). The former enables a more accurate assessment of the importance of particular species in the vegetation and enables a distinction to be made between actual fluctuations of a species and those caused as a result of the fluctuations of another. Three-dimensional pollen diagrams involve the location of precisely contemporary horizons in a peat bog at several points over a wide area and the comparison of pollen spectra from these points. In this way a more accurate estimation of the location of the areas affected by particular land-use effects, as well as the size of the area involved, can be determined.

Macroscopic plant remains (Dimbleby, 1967)

Under the heading of macroscopic plant remains is included a whole variety of bits and pieces ranging from massive tree trunks, stumps and branches to minute seeds often smaller than a pin-head. Their main value is in the interpretation of local features of the environment. Their preservation occurs only under anaerobic conditions such as peat bogs, waterlogged ditches and wells. (Special cases such as casts, charcoal and so forth, are considered later.)

The best known occurrence of macroscopic plant remains are the tree stools preserved *in situ* in peat bogs (Fig.46) and around the coast as submerged forests (Fig.35). Intervening layers may consist of plant remains preserved to a greater or lesser degree — twigs and branches, reeds, and *Sphagnum* moss (p.107) — and different types of peat are often named by their most characteristic plant remains. Study of these can yield a picture of the local environmental changes which took place as the peat bog built up (Fig.45). Prior to the discovery of pollen analysis these vegetational layers were used to construct what was thought to be a climatically controlled succession of periods covering the last 10,000 years in north-west Europe (Blytt, 1876; Sernander, 1908) (Table 5). Horizons of rapid peat growth were considered to reflect periods of relatively oceanic climate, horizons of tree stumps or wood peat periods of relatively continental climate, and it was from this kind of evidence that the succession of Pre-boreal, Boreal, Atlantic, Sub-boreal and Sub-atlantic periods was constructed. Although this scheme still provides a useful framework for the Flandrian, and although many of its climatic implications are still valid, pollen analysis has shown that many of the tree stool horizons — particularly in their species composition — are local features peculiar to the bog environment (Birks, 1975). Moreover, radiocarbon dating has invalidated the general synchroneity of the scheme over a wide area (Smith and Pilcher, 1973).

Macroscopic plant remains — particularly leaves, twigs and seeds — are common on waterlogged archaeological sites of the *ditch*, *pit* and *well* category (Fig.49). River gravel areas are especially conducive to the creation of conditions suitable for the preservation of organic material. Bulk samples of sediment are generally taken, and the remains extracted in the laboratory. Alternatively, various on-site flotation machines can be used, a system which has become increasingly popular in recent years (Jarman, *et al.*, 1972). This involves three stages. First, the sediment is broken down as finely as possible. Second, paraffin is added which selectively coats organic particles and increases their surface tension. Third, a detergent is added and the mixture agitated to create a froth; this causes the paraffin-coated particles to float — the detergent bubbles being selectively attracted to the paraffin surfaces. Organic material is thus concentrated at the surface of the mixture and can be skimmed off, dried and sorted. The technique is known as *froth flotation.*

Identification and study are a specialist business. A large reference collection of the various groups of plant debris is essential, together with a sound botanical knowledge. Interpretation — as with most other macroscopic material from archaeological sites — must take into account the way in which the remains found their way, first onto the site, and second into the deposit. What this implies in practice is an assessment of whether the plant remains were intrinsic to the vegetation of the site or brought in by man. In the first category we may expect to find remains of plants which were (a) growing in or very close to the feature in which they were deposited, and (b) growing a few metres away. The boundary ditch of a field, for example, might be expected to yield the seeds of aquatic or marsh plants growing in or alongside the ditch, twigs and seeds of shrubs growing along the edge of the ditch, and the seeds of weed species and also cereal grains of plants growing in the ambient fields (Fig.7).

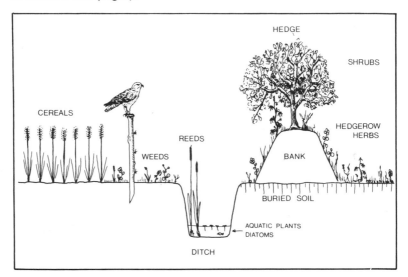

Fig.7. Transverse section of a bank and ditch showing the various habitats from which plant remains may be derived and incorporated into the ditch deposits. The different habitats will also support their own individual insect, snail and small mammal faunas, all of which will eventually come together as a death assemblage in the ditch bottom.

Plants brought in by man include firewood and artefacts such as handles, fence posts and so forth. This category of material is generally more important on occupation sites.

Macroscopic plant remains have also been found in the stomach contents of human bog burials (Glob, 1969) and frozen mammoths, but these clearly are not of general relevance. Coprolites (p.61) and other situations in which dryness inhibits microbial decay are additional sources of plant material.

Charcoal (Dimbleby, 1967)

Charcoal is practically ubiquitous on archaeological sites. It is always burnt organic material, with a high percentage of elemental carbon. It is generally derived from wood or grain. Its ubiquity is due to the fact that it is largely mineral and thus indestructible by microbial activity.

The origins of charcoal — as of the macroscopic plant remains already discussed — may be various, and the following categories can be recognized:

(1) Burning off of vegetation by man or natural means.
(2) Firewood, involving the selection of particular species for their kindling/burning properties.
(3) Artefacts.
(4) Remnants of structural timbers burnt *in situ*.
(5) Grain, accidentally charred while drying.

In the interpretation of charcoal remains, therefore, care must be exercised in deciding which of these various processes and origins are involved. Widespread charcoal horizons such as occur on Palaeolithic and Mesolithic sites are likely to fall into category (1) and be representative of the vegetation of the area as a whole. Hearth sites in caves or open-air situations are more likely to have a high percentage of artificially selected species (category 2). Occupation horizons — the fill of pits for instance — are likely to contain material of categories (3) and (5), again artificially selected. And burnt timbers of category (4) are likely in upstanding monuments and post-holes.

Interpretation of charcoal remains has been discussed by several workers with reference to Flandrian climatic and environmental conditions on the chalklands of southern Britain (Godwin and Tansley, 1941). For example, willow charcoal has been recovered from Neolithic flint mines on the Chalk. This could be — and has been — interpreted as reflecting damper *climatic* conditions on the Chalk in Neolithic times. But it is more probable that the willow wood was used in the manufacture of baskets for lifting the flint nodules to the surface, and derives ultimately from some lowlying area of damper *environment* ambient to the uplands.

Impressions (Dimbleby, 1967)

Impressions of plant remains occur in various circumstances on archaeological sites and in environmental contexts. An impression forms when a plant becomes incorporated into a plastic material like clay and is subsequently destroyed leaving the details of the surface morphology. The following materials are the most likely to yield impressions:

(1) Mud brick (p.125).
(2) Pottery.
(3) Tile.
(4) Tufa and stalagmite (p.71).

The reliability of the evidence for environmental interpretation depends on the way in which the plant remains become incorporated, and on the material in which the impressions are formed. For example, impressions in tufa will probably derive from the natural marsh or swamp vegetation in which the deposit was accumulating. Stalagmite, too, will yield data about the natural vegetation, but specific to the local environment of a cave. Pottery and tile, on the other hand, usually preserve evidence of domestic practices — particularly cereal impressions — and are not so useful in environmental work. Impressions in mud brick may derive from (a) plants incorporated accidentally during the collecting of the mud, (b) plant material — particularly grass stems — put in deliberately to strengthen the bricks and to prevent cracking, and (c) plants incorporated accidentally during drying, these generally from the occupation area.

Cereal impressions (and charred grain) have been used to interpret the main types of prehistoric farming practice (Helbaek, 1952; 1969). In Britain, for example, it was considered, until recently, that wheats were important in Neolithic and Iron Age times, while barley was more important during the Bronze Age. Environmentally, this has sometimes been linked to the supposed dampness of climate during Neolithic and Iron Age times and the supposed dryness of climate during the Bronze Age. It has now been suggested, however, that there was an equal dependence on these two cereal crops throughout the period of prehistoric farming and that any differences were of a regional nature (Dennell, 1976a).

Phytoliths (Dimbleby, 1967)

Phytoliths, or plant opals, are microscopic silica bodies which occur within the cells of certain plants, particularly the grasses (Fig.8). They are sometimes concentrated along leaf margins, as in the sword grasses, where they are responsible for the very sharp edge. The gloss which is a feature of flint sickle blades is caused by constant wear against these silica bodies during reaping. The study of phytoliths is not well advanced and the conditions under which they are preserved are not well known. They are identified by their shape and size (Fig.8), although some are not diagnostic to species. Also, two or more forms may occur in a single species, depending

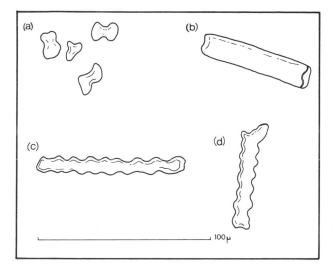

Fig.8. Phytoliths. (a) Dumbell form. Purple moor-grass (*Molinia caerulea*). (b) Simple rod form. Wall barley (*Hordium murinum*). (c) Wavy-edged rod form. Sweet vernal-grass (*Anthoxanthum odoratum*). (d) Wavy-edged rod form. Cock's-foot (*Dactylis glomerata*). (From Dimbleby, 1967)

on the type of cell from which they derive. Phytoliths have been extracted from archaeological deposits, particularly the ashy fills of pits and hearths. Other parts of the silica skeleton of plants may also occur.

Diatoms

Diatoms are microscopic unicellular or colonial Algae which live in aquatic habitats — freshwater, estuarine and marine. The cell wall is of silica and it is because of this that the organisms are preserved in ancient sediments. Thick deposits consisting largely of diatoms formed during various geological periods; these are known as 'diatomaceous earth' and are mined for various purposes — notably for use in the manufacture of dynamite. There are many different species and identification is based on form, size and the sculpturing of the cell wall (Fig.9).

On the whole, each species is confined to a particular habitat, and the group is especially useful in the study of coastal sediments for determining salinity. For example, in Denmark diatoms have shown the presence of four successive stages in the Flandrian trans-

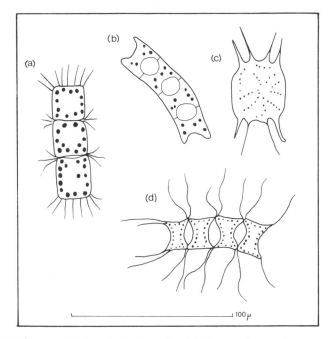

Fig.9. Diatoms. (a) *Lauderia borealis*. (b) *Eucampia zoodiacus*.
(c) *Biddulphia mobiliensis*. (d) *Chaetoceros curvisetus*. All are marine
species. (From Russell and Yonge, 1936)

gression of the sea (Clark, 1975). Considerable work has also been
done in Holland. One of the earliest studies was on the Late-
Devensian and Flandrian diatom succession of the Windermere
bottom deposits in the English Lake District (Fig.10) (Pennington,
1943).

Dendrochronology (Bannister, 1969; Dimbleby, 1967)

A rather special application of timber remains to environmental
research is tree-ring analysis or dendrochronology. This is generally
used as a dating technique but it can provide valuable environmental and climatic data as well. The method is based on the fact
that trees lay down one growth ring of cells annually — large cells
in spring and early summer, small cells in late summer and autumn,
with cessation of growth during winter (Fig.11). This, of course,
applies only to regions with strongly seasonal climate. The thickness of the rings is, in some cases, climatically controlled — by

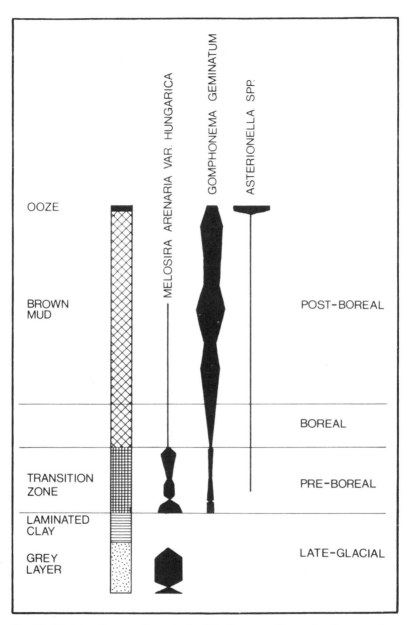

Fig.10. Diatom diagram from Lake Windermere. Generalized curves for three species of diatom showing the vertical distribution through Late-Devensian and Flandrian deposits. (From Pennington, 1943)

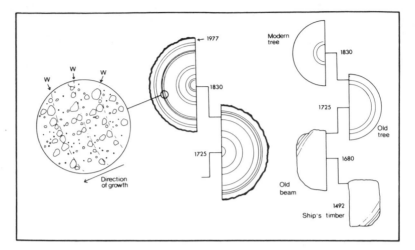

Fig.11. Dendrochronology. The principle of cross-dating. On the left, an enlarged section of timber showing four annual rings with their different sized cells; w=winter standstill. In the centre, the matching of two trees of different ages. On the right, extension of the cross-dating principle to old structural timbers.

temperature or moisture in different instances — and the pattern of varying thicknesses through a tree trunk may be taken as an indication of the variations in climate during the life of the tree.

The method is only useful, of course, if the individual rings can be dated. This can be done by working backwards from timber of known date, matching the patterns of variation, a process known as *cross-dating* (Fig.12). Sequences have been produced from parts of Europe going back into medieval times, as at the city of Novgorod the Great (Thompson, 1967), and have provided information about climatic change during the period (Schove and Lowther, 1957). In some cases a sequence of cross-dated timbers may be determined but without the link to the present day. This is known as a *floating chronology*, and is of value in tying in buildings or other structures to a relative sequence. The timber trackways of the Somerset Levels are a case in point (Coles, *et al.*, 1975).

A special instance of the use of dendrochronology is in the checking of radiocarbon dating (Renfrew, 1973). The bristlecone pine, *Pinus aristata*, grows in the White Mountains of California, and many examples of the tree are thousands of years old. Dead trees decay very slowly and their timber can be tied in by cross-dating to the living trees. In this way a very long sequence of dated timber

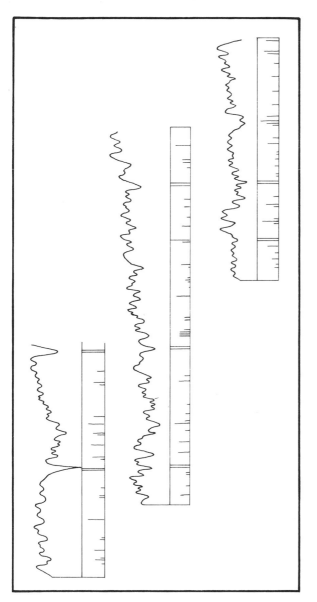

Fig.12. Dendrochronology. Method of linking graphs of growth rings from three timbers of different ages but with overlapping sections. Only exceptionally thin rings, shown by the horizontal bars, are used in the matching process. Novgorod the Great. (From Thompson, 1967)

extending well beyond 5000 B.C. has been established. Radiocarbon assay of this material has produced dates which err on the young side — towards the early end of the scale by almost a millennium (Fig.13). This suggests that the production of radiocarbon in the upper atmosphere has not always been constant, and that more was being formed 7,000 years ago than today. The precise reason for this is not clear but may be linked to the amount of radiation being received by the earth, and thus to climate. Minor variations in recent centuries can be linked to sunspot activity. In other words the variations in the production of radiocarbon may have an environmental basis that could be used for checking and augmenting the evidence of past climatic change from the more conventional biological data.

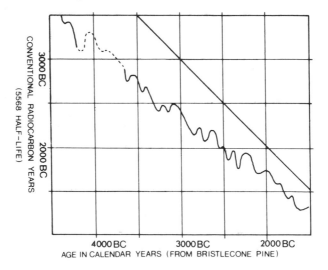

Fig.13. Comparison between theoretical (straight line) and actual (irregular line) graphs for the radiocarbon assay of bristlecone pine timber. (Based on the work of H. E. Suess, and taken from Renfrew, 1973)

Other groups of plants

The occurrence of plant remains has been dealt with largely on a basis of categories of plant parts and types of preservation. It will be useful to conclude with a brief section on certain taxonomic groups. These are as follows:

Seaweeds
Other Algae
Mosses
Ferns and bracken
Fungi
Bacteria and viruses

Evidence for the presence of *seaweeds* in archaeological contexts is usually indirect. Seaweed was, and still is, collected by coastal peoples for manuring the land and for the manufacture of kelp — a dried and burnt product rich in chlorides, iodides and other salts. It was used in the manufacture of glass, soap and munitions. Certain species of mollusc live preferentially on the fronds and holdfasts of the kelp seaweeds; notable in Britain are the flat winkle, *Littorina littoralis* (Fig.21), and the blue-rayed limpet, *Patina pellucida*. Neither of these species is large enough or sufficiently abundant to be worth collecting for food, and their presence in an archaeological context may be taken as indicating the possibility of seaweed collecting. Burnt shells of these species are even more convincing as evidence of kelping. Such were recovered during recent excavations on the Isles of Scilly from an eighteenth century site for which there was documentary evidence for kelping. It should be mentioned that *Littorina littoralis* was also used extensively in prehistoric times for beads, but the perforated shell betrays this function.

Apart from the diatoms already discussed, a few groups of *other Algae* may be found. The female organs or oogonia of various stoneworts, *Chara* spp., have often been recorded from warm-climate freshwater deposits (e.g. Kelly, 1968). About the size of a small pin-head, these oval or barrel-shaped calcareous bodies are readily recognizable by the fine spiral thickening of the wall. The oogonia form under adverse conditions such as temporary drought. Spores of various freshwater green Algae, for example *Spirogyra*, have been recovered from the ditch fill of a Bronze Age settlement in the Netherlands (van Geel, 1976).

Mosses or Bryophytes are widely reported from Pleistocene deposits (Dickson, 1973), less so from archaeological sites. In some instances, as with the moss flora from the turf-stack of Silbury Hill, mosses can provide fairly detailed information about the past environment (Williams, 1976). At this site, the species indicated the existence of moderately grazed mature chalk grassland, and that the turves originated from a north-facing slope. In other instances, as at Roman Vindolanda (Seaward and Williams, 1976), the mosses were brought onto the site by man for various purposes such as bedding, packing, insulation, absorption and caulking.

Occurrences of *ferns* or Pteridophytes fall into the same two categories — naturally occurring on site or brought in by man. Spores of ferns, and in particular bracken, are common in pollen-bearing deposits. They are especially characteristic of buried soils, where their abundance may be due to their better preservation than the pollen of higher plants. Records of bracken from Neolithic sites on the Chalk of southern Britain are curious in view of the absence of the species from pure chalk soils at the present day (Dimbleby and Evans, 1974). It is possible that the bracken was used as bedding for cattle and then mucked out onto the fields as manure.

Fungi may occur either as macroscopic fruiting bodies, particularly those of the very resistant bracket-fungus group, or as microscopic filaments and spores. Spores of the puff-ball, *Bovista nigrescens*, are recorded from Roman deposits at Vindolanda and Neolithic deposits at Skara Brae, Orkney. In a number of cases it is likely that fungi were imported to a site by man. They have many functions. Puff-balls were a delicacy, eaten in Roman times. They can also be used for medicinal purposes, for tinder, or for their hallucinogenic properties. Some fungi, notably the stink-horn, *Phallus impudicus*, have a phallic appearance and may have been collected as cult objects (Watling and Seaward, 1976).

Records of *bacteria and viruses* are mostly indirect through the effect of their diseases in man and animals. Tuberculosis, leprosy, yaws and syphilis are all known from early times from their effect on bone (Brothwell, 1972). An engraving on an Egyptian stele, dating from the thirteenth century B.C., shows a man with a withered and shortened leg, and is probably the earliest known record of poliomyelitis (Wells, 1964).

3 Animal remains

As with plants, animal remains on archaeological sites may derive from various sources, and it is important that these be assessed before any judgement about former environments be made. Most problems arise with those animals that were used as food or for other purposes — e.g. traction — by man, for then there is generally the chance that selection of one or a few species took place. Human food debris need not be — and generally is not — a true reflection of the relative abundance of the various species in the wild, and must therefore be used with caution in determining ancient environments. Moreover, even within one human group, the nature of the food debris may vary according to the type of site or situation. For example, in a hunting community a kill site might have bones of only the larger animals — those that were too heavy to transport; a home base, on the other hand, would have only the smaller animals — those that could be carried back whole from the kill. The season of occupation of a site is also important. Some animals are migratory, and a site occupied during only one season — even if successively over a number of years — might lack whole sections of the fauna.

Animals may also be incorporated into deposits by other animals, and this applies particularly to caves and fissures. Carnivorous forms such as hyenas, lions and bears may take all or part of their prey back to their den, and if the site is occupied by man also — even if alternately with the carnivores — it may be difficult to distinguish the debris of human from animal meals (Fig.14). Birds of prey regurgitate pellets made up of small mammal bones — largely rodents — and these often occur in vast numbers beneath their roosts, which are usually caves or cliffs but may sometimes be open-air sites where a fence, for example, was constructed. Shell-fish, too, may be gathered by sea birds and the empty shells dropped on land. There is also the strong possibility that animals, as well as man, hunted their prey selectively, concentrating not only on particular species but also on limited age ranges and sex. Again, therefore, the debris of these meals is not likely to be totally representative of the natural population.

The third way in which animal remains become incorporated into deposits is that they actually lived — and died — on the site. Here

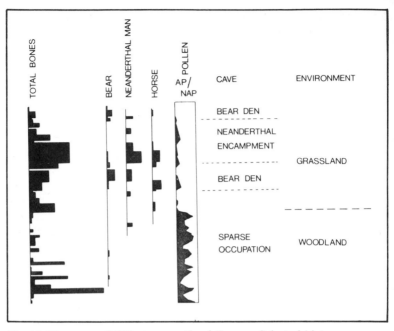

Fig.14. The cave of l'Hortus, south of France. Selected histograms through the Neanderthal deposits, for bones and pollen. The cave (local) and general environment are indicated. (From de Lumley, 1972)

we are on slightly safer ground in utilizing the fauna to reconstruct the environment, but there are still problems. The nature of the site controls to some extent the nature of the fauna. Cave sites, for example, are often rich in carnivore remains out of all proportion to the abundance of the creatures in the wild. River gravel deposits are generally rich in herbivores. On archaeological sites, invertebrates, and particularly slow-moving creatures like snails, often strongly reflect micro-climates — for example in the bottom of a ditch or well. Even the general nature of the environment may be modified by man, and this be reflected in the fauna. The problems of generalizing from specific faunal assemblages are difficult.

To summarize, animal remains may become incorporated into deposits in one of three ways:

(1) They are the product of human food debris.
(2) They are the product of animal food debris.
(3) They were living on the site.

Evolution and faunal change (Kurtén, 1968; Zeuner, 1959)

There is a further introductory point that needs clarification. In using animals as evidence of past environments we are applying the principles outlined at the beginning of Chapter 2, namely that present-day geographical ranges and habitats are the basis for our interpretation. Faunal changes through the Pleistocene are in the *distribution and abundance* of species which are alive today or which, if extinct, were closely related to living forms. Only in a very few instances — notably certain groups of mammals, including man — are we dealing with *evolutionary change*. The elephants, for example, have evolved from fairly generalized omnivorous forms to highly specialized creatures like the mammoth adapted to living in extreme cold and eating the tough, siliceous, vegetation of steppe and tundra. The changing form of *Bison* species through the American Pleistocene is another example of evolution (Fig.15).

Large mammals (Chaplin, 1971; Cornwall, 1956; Kurtén, 1968)

The remains of large mammals — as of vertebrates generally — are almost invariably skeletal. Only under exceptional conditions of preservation are other animal tissues preserved. These, however, have yielded some of our most spectacular discoveries and are worth a mention. Mummification and extreme *dryness* have led to the preservation of the bodies of humans and animals in Egyptian tombs. *Permafrost* conditions in Siberia have preserved whole carcasses of mammoth; and the bodies of woolly rhinoceros have been preserved in *brine* deposits in Poland. In north-west Europe, particularly in Denmark, a number of bodies of Iron Age men have been recovered intact with hair and stomach contents, having been preserved in peat bogs under *anaerobic* conditions — aided perhaps by *tanning* of the skin by peat exudates. Leather is sometimes recovered from waterlogged deposits, especially in town sites (p.124).

The large size of many animal bones presents problems both of a mechanical nature and of obtaining a large enough sample for the result to be statistically meaningful. The study of creatures such as elephants and hippos has to be done largely in the field, particularly if working in isolated areas. Only under exceptional conditions are resources available for the lifting of whole skeletons of these animals and their removal to a laboratory for study.

The study of animal bones takes place in several stages. First of all, as many bone fragments as possible are *identified*. This yields a

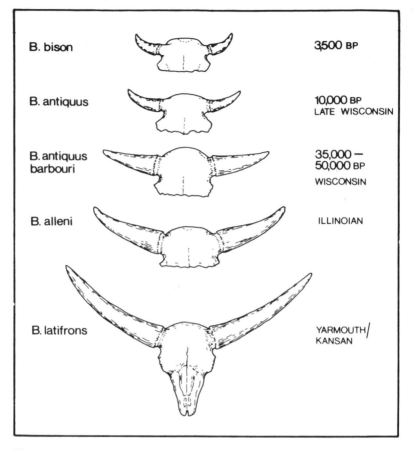

Fig.15. The changing form of *Bison* species as shown by skulls from deposits in the Central Great Plains, U.S.A. (See Table 3, p.131, for Pleistocene stages.) The earliest skull is at the base. (From Schultz and Martin, 1970)

species list but the relative abundance of fragments will almost certainly not be a reflection of the true structure of the fauna. Some species will be over-represented due to the counting of more than one bone from the same animal.

The second stage is the estimation of the *minimum number* of individuals of each species. This is done by counting only one specific bone — for example the hind upper limb bone, or femur — and will give a more accurate reflection of the abundance of the various animals in the fauna. If sufficient numbers are present —

150 examples is a useful standard (although seldom achieved) — the results can be expressed in percentage terms.

Environmental reconstruction, based on a consideration of present-day habitats and geographical ranges, can then follow. This is not always a good guide but is usually all there is to go on. The present-day ranges of many species are controlled by man either in creating habitats unsuitable for them or by active extermination. For example, species such as the lion and the elephant are quite capable of surviving in the more temperate regions of western Europe today, and, although now confined more or less to the tropics, their presence in Britain during former interglacials is no indication of tropical climate during those times. Another problem is that the larger mammals are very adaptable and can occupy a wide range of habitats. Furthermore, some species occur in several different behavioural and ecological varieties known as *ecotypes* which show no morphological differences and yet occupy different habitats. An additional problem arises with extinct species. Here one has to use what morphological clues are available as to habitat and mode of life, as well as building up a picture from other evidence — associated fauna, soils, sediments and plant remains.

Table 1. Changes in the deer fauna during the Late-Devensian and Flandrian periods in Britain.

Historical period	Introduction of various foreign species e.g. *Muntjak*, *Chinese Water Deer* and *Sika*, mainly in the twentieth century. Re-introduction of the *Reindeer*.
Roman period	Introduction of the *Fallow Deer*.
Mid-Flandrian Deciduous woodland	*Red* and *Roe Deer* predominant. Associated woodland fauna of pig and wild ox.
Early-Flandrian Birch/pine woodland	*Elk* characteristic, with *Red* and *Roe Deer*. Associated woodland fauna.
Late-Devensian zones II and III	*Giant Irish Deer* and *Reindeer* with associated cold-climate fauna.
Late-Devensian zone I	*Reindeer* with associated cold-climate fauna.

With all the problems intrinsic to the faunal assemblages themselves, as well as those concerning the mode of incorporation of the remains into a deposit, it is clearly desirable to use large collections in order that the results at least be statistically valid even although their interpretation may be unclear. In spite of all the difficulties, however, we do have a fairly clear idea of the broad outline of faunal change during the Pleistocene in various parts of the world. Table 1 shows some of the changes that have taken place during the later part of the Devensian and Flandrian periods in Britain with special reference to the deer.

Further study of animal remains involves the *distribution of sexes* in the population, and the various *age ranges*. Both can indicate, for example, whether a species was domesticated or wild, and the pattern of exploitation of the species by man. Measurements of particular bones can be plotted as scatter diagrams (Fig.16) and used to separate the sexes and closely related species.

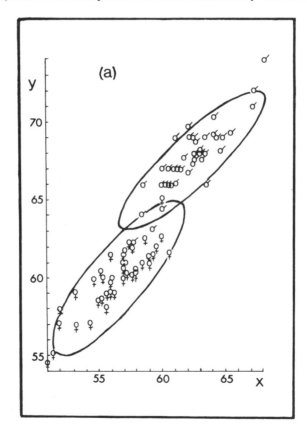

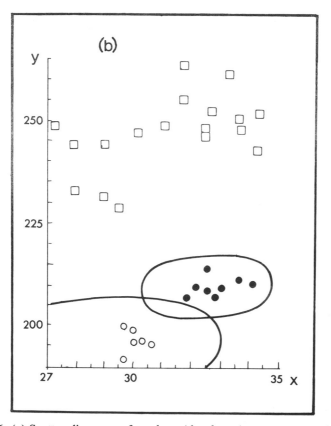

Fig.16. (a) Scatter diagrams of modern Aberdeen Angus metacarpals (lower limb or cannon bone). Y-axis, maximum distal width; X-axis, maximum distal diaphysial width. Specimens from cows (♀) and steers (♂). Notice that, although there is overlap of the two groups, by measuring a sufficient number of examples the distinction between the two sexes is clear. (b) Scatter diagram of Danish prehistoric cattle metacarpals. Y-axis, maximum length; X-axis, ratio of distal width to length. Squares=wild ox (*Bos primigenius*); circles=non-wild ox cattle; open circles=females; blacked circles=steers. (From Higham, 1969)

A striking example of a very definite pattern of exploitation comes from the Klasies River Mouth Cave in southern Africa, a Middle Stone Age site. Bone remains of the African giant buffalo — a very ferocious species — showed a predominance of mature females and very young, frequently foetal, individuals. Clearly the section of the population being exploited consisted mainly of females in a very advanced state of pregnancy or just having given birth, in both cases animals encumbered and unable to exercise their usual aggression (Klein, 1975).

Evidence for the season of occupation of a site by man can also be got from a study of animal bones. Since, however, there are other animal groups besides the mammals that can yield this data, the evidence as a whole is brought together at the end of this chapter (p.62).

An unusual and fascinating source of information about animal communities is prehistoric rock art, particularly that from the later Stone Age cave sites of Ice Age Europe (Ucko and Rosenfeld, 1967). Here are represented, often in beautiful polychrome paintings, the various species of animal hunted by man. Not only can we get some idea of faunal assemblages (Fig.17) but also of species long extinct like the mammoth, woolly rhino and giant deer.

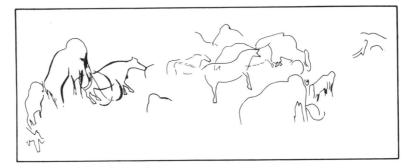

Fig.17. Frieze of animals in the cave of Pech Merle, France, painted in Upper Palaeolithic times. The animals include wild ox, mammoth, horse and bison.

However, it must be remembered that the grouping of animals on cave walls may be determined by magical, religious or symbolic considerations and may not be a true reflection of natural assemblages. The reindeer, for example, although widely hunted in the Upper Palaeolithic, is poorly represented in cave art.

Human bones

Some information about the environment can be got from a study of human bones, particularly with regard to ancient diseases (p.34) and diet (Brothwell, 1972; Brothwell and Brothwell, 1969). For example, lack of vitamin D and calcium causes rickets, various symptoms of which may occur in bone. These include general retardation of skeletal growth, light and brittle bones, and the bowing of the long bones, especially the femur. Dental decay is also related to diet.

The human skeleton is the closest we come to man in prehistory and one would suppose that its study would be the hub of research into the human environment. There has, however, been remarkably little work done on the effects of various environmental factors on man's skeletal remains. This is a wide open field.

Small mammals

At any rate in north-west Europe, small mammals include mainly rodents — voles, mice, lemmings and so on — although other animals such as insectivores (shrew and hedgehog) and the smaller carnivores (pine marten, polecat and weasel) also occur. Their main value is in environmental reconstruction, and it is unlikely that they were commonly eaten by man. They occur in a wide variety of sites, although caves and fissures are the most common, and it is probable that major accumulations of small rodent bones are due to birds of prey. However, it has been suggested that the concentrations of small mammal bones found associated with hominid remains at Olduvai Gorge in East Africa derive from human dung (Sampson, 1974). That this is certainly a possibility was shown by L. S. B. Leakey by direct experiment.

Material for small mammal analysis is collected in a variety of ways:

(1) Larger bones are picked out during excavation.
(2) On-site sieving.
(3) Collection of soil samples and their sorting in the laboratory. A 0·5 mm mesh is essential for the bones of smaller shrews and rodents.
(4) Flotation techniques (p.23), used on site or in the laboratory.

Identification is best done on teeth and skull fragments. Limb bones are less suitable; ribs and vertebrae are very difficult to identify indeed.

As with the larger species, small mammals can give information about contemporary climate and vegetation cover, although it is sometimes difficult to separate these two. Woodland habitats generally support a large variety of species by comparison with open habitats such as grassland and tundra. On the other hand, the number of individuals per unit area may be greater in open habitats. But as indicators of the precise nature of the vegetation small mammals are often less reliable than the larger species due to the fact that similar micro-habitats can be created by widely diverse vegetation types, particularly the various types of woodland understorey. On the other hand, present geographical ranges are more reliable as indicators of climatic tolerance than is the case with the larger mammals, since there is a greater number of residual niches which provide suitable habitats, even in the heavily farmed countries of western Europe.

In Britain, the bones of various species of lemming and vole occur in cold-climate deposits from the Devensian Glaciation and earlier periods (Stuart, 1976). From Flandrian deposits there are rich woodland faunas at various early sites, for example Star Carr in north-east Yorkshire where pine marten, fox, badger and hedgehog occurred along with larger woodland species (Clark, 1954). Faunas from Neolithic flint mines in the south include woodland species of bat. Buried soils under Neolithic monuments have yielded a sequence of two faunal assemblages which can be equated with the evidence of land snails (p.56). The earlier of these consists of a variety of species — mice, shrews and the bank vole — which occur in conjunction with a snail fauna indicative of woodland. The later assemblage, occurring in conjunction with a grassland snail fauna, consists of only the field vole. On open-air Bronze Age sites concentrations of small mammal bones have been taken as indicative of upstanding structures such as fences, rings of posts or totem poles, on which birds of prey perched while regurgitating their pellets. Water vole remains are common on lowlying sites of the ditch, pit and well category.

Outside Britain, large numbers of species have been recovered from cave and fissure deposits, for example from the Australopithecine sites in southern Africa (Sampson, 1974). But little detailed work has yet been done on these.

Birds (Dawson, 1969)

On the whole, bird remains have not been studied to the same extent as mammals, due largely to difficulties of identification — lack of reference material — and their small size. The following categories may occur:

(1) Bones.
(2) Feathers, claws and beaks in exceptional conditions of preservation.

(3) Egg shell.
(4) Guano (excreta).
(5) Pellets.

Bones, feathers and egg shell may become incorporated into soils and sediments in one or more of the various ways discussed on p.35. Guano and pellets constitute evidence of the immediate presence of birds.

On archaeological sites, bird bones and egg shell indicate which species and which environments were available to, and were being exploited by, man. Migratory species, particularly in the northern hemisphere, can be, and have been, used to indicate the time of year a site was occupied (p.62). The massing of hundreds of thousands of wild fowl for their autumn or spring migrations, or the concentration of gulls during the nesting season, almost certainly provided a readily exploitable source of food for early man. Today, the vast numbers of birds can only really be appreciated on the more remote uninhabited islands or extensive mud flats. Even so, some species, such as the great auk and the moa, have been hunted to extinction by man, in the case of the moa necessitating 'a reorientation of food-getting habits with fish replacing bird' (Brothwell and Brothwell, 1969).

Reptiles and Amphibia

This category includes turtles, snakes and crocodiles (the reptiles), and frogs, toads and salamanders (the amphibians). Remains of these creatures occur very infrequently on archaeological sites and have been little studied. In Britain, perhaps most usual are the bones of frogs from the waterlogged fills of wells and ditches, although they also occur on more terrestrial sites such as the high downland chalk and in caves. Outside Britain and northern Europe, where there are larger species, reptile and amphibian remains are more commonly recorded — for example in southern Africa (Sampson, 1974) — but they have been little used in environmental work.

One animal however needs special mention, the European pond tortoise, *Emys orbicularis*. *Emys* occurred in Britain and Europe during the Flandrian and previous interglacials well to the north and west of its present breeding range (Degerbøl and Krog, 1951). This supports other biological evidence for warmer, and perhaps more continental, climatic conditions during these periods than obtain today.

Fish (Casteel, 1976b; Ryder, 1969)

Fish remains are of three kinds: (a) bones, (b) otoliths, and (c) scales. The fish *skeleton* is complex, particularly the skull which generally breaks up into a number of separate units. Most easily identifiable are the jaw bones and teeth; vertebrae and other elements are more difficult, but possible with good reference material. *Otoliths* — ear stones — are particularly useful. They are generally identifiable to species. Moreover they have the particular characteristic (along with the vertebrae and scales) of growing in annual rings (Fig.18) so that they can be used to age the fish, and to indicate whether or not a site was occupied on a seasonal basis. Unfortunately they have rarely been recorded from archaeological sites, although there are notable exceptions as in the case of various coastal Indian sites in California. *Scales* are rarely found except under anaerobic conditions or in very recent deposits. They too are often identifiable to species.

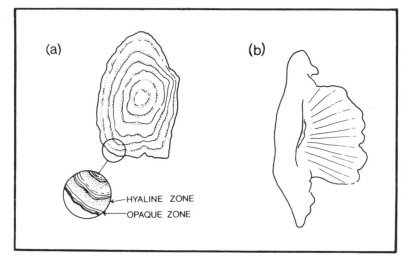

Fig.18. Fish otoliths. (a) Plaice, *Pleuronectes platessa*. (b) Angler, *Lophius piscatorius*. Both × 4. In the plaice otolith the annual growth increments are clearly visible, the hyaline zone corresponding to winter growth, the opaque zone to spring and summer growth. Within the opaque zone finer increments are visible.

Fish occupy a wide variety of habitats and are potentially useful as indicators of ancient river hydrology, the environment of accumulation of a deposit, the environments exploited by man, and the season of occupation of a site. The main groups are marine, estuarine and freshwater, and within each group finer distinctions can be made. In the marine group for example, rock pool, rocky coast, sandy coast and deep sea can be recognized, while in the freshwater group the main division is between species of well-oxygenated habitats such as large lakes and rivers, and species of poorly-oxygenated habitats such as ponds, sluggish rivers, back-swamp areas and so on. The exploitation of deep-sea species like cod as well as marine mammals such as dolphin, seal and killer whale, implies considerable hunting skill and the use of boats. The exploitation of anadromous species like the salmon — species which spend part of their life cycle in freshwater and part in the sea — may be used in some instances to indicate the season of occupation of a site.

In Britain, fish remains have been recorded from Pleistocene deposits as at Upton Warren, Worcestershire (Coope, *et al.*, 1961) and Minchin Hole Cave, Gower. In the former case they were probably coeval with the deposits which were indicative of small pools on a river flood plain. In the latter they had probably been brought in by seabirds and regurgitated onto a land surface in pellets. In both cases the species was the three-spined stickleback.

Fish remains also occur in archaeological deposits where they are most likely human food debris. One of the best studied sites is Galatea Bay, New Zealand (Shawcross, 1967). Considerable work has been done on Russian sites and some of this has been briefly discussed by Casteel (1976b).

Probably the main reason for the sparseness of records of fish remains from archaeological sites — particularly in Britain — is their small size. Sieving techniques in use over the last few years have greatly increased the number of instances in which fish remains have been reported (Casteel, 1976a).

Insects (Buckland, 1976; Coope, 1967)

All subsequent animal remains to be considered are *invertebrates*, and the two main groups as far as occurrence on archaeological sites is concerned are the insects and the molluscs.

Lest there be any confusion — and there generally is — insects are invertebrates with six legs and a body composed of three parts, head, thorax and abdomen. Typical insects are beetles, wasps, ants, moths and locusts. The group does not include worms, snails, spiders or woodlice (Buchsbaum, 1951).

Insect remains occur almost exclusively in anaerobic deposits — peats, muds, and the lower layers of archaeological features such as ditches, wells and sewers; they are especially common in towns. They are rare in buried soils, an exception being the vast prehistoric monument of Silbury Hill in north Wiltshire, where the extreme thickness of the mound had completely excluded the atmosphere from the original ground surface; in consequence a fauna including ant, beetle and grasshopper remains was preserved. On the whole it is the horny (chitinous) exoskeleton of beetles that is most commonly found — the wing cases (or elytra), the thorax, head, mouth-parts and legs — but other parts (e.g. actual wings) and other groups sometimes occur.

The extraction procedure is straightforward and similar in principle to the froth flotation method described for seeds. The use of on-site machines, however, is not popular, and samples of sediment are generally broken down in the laboratory. The use of paraffin and gentle frothing yields an insect-rich flotant which can be skimmed off and examined. Identification is less easy, due to the large number of species and to the fact that features used in the identification of modern specimens are not always preserved subfossil. A good reference collection is essential.

Insect faunas can yield information of importance to the archaeologist in three categories:

(1) Climate.
(2) Regional and local environment.
(3) Economy.

Beetles are particularly important because many species live in very precisely defined habitats and yet the group as a whole covers a very wide range. Some species are phytophagous (plant eaters), some carnivores, and some feed on dung. A whole variety of aquatic and terrestrial habitats is occupied — open-water, water edge, grassland, forest canopy, forest floor, dead wood and so on — and some species can be identified with specific processes like grain storage or tanning.

A number of species found in Pleistocene deposits no longer occur in Britain (Fig.19), and these provide useful indices of past climates. Indeed, insects are of particular value in climatic interpretation in that they react more quickly to climate change than do plants. This has been demonstrated very clearly in studies of the Late-Devensian in Britain (Coope and Brophy, 1972). The period of maximum climatic amelioration, formerly thought to be zone II (Table 5), has been shown through insect studies to have been late zone I, a period when the vegetation was still largely treeless. Zone II, on the other hand, a period of birch woodland in sheltered

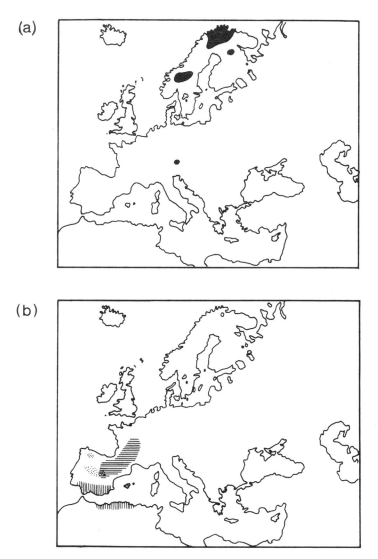

Fig.19. Present-day European distribution of beetle species formerly occurring in Britain during the Pleistocene. (a) *Syncalypta cyclolepida*, recorded from cold-climate early zone I Late-Devensian deposits in North Wales (From Coope and Brophy, 1972). (b) *Aphodius bonvouloiri* (stippled), *Cathormiocerus curviscapus* (vertical lines) and *Cathormiocerus validiscapus* (horizontal lines), recorded from mid-Devensian deposits in southern Britain. (From Coope and Angus, 1975)

places at least, in fact witnessed a temperature decline. Osborne (1976), studying insect remains from Flandrian deposits, has suggested a new model for temperature changes during the period (Fig.20). Instead of the slow rise to an 'optimum' followed by a decline, he has suggested a rapid rise to the present-day values which is maintained except for short periods of decline. The latter correlate with readvances of Alpine glaciers. However, it should be

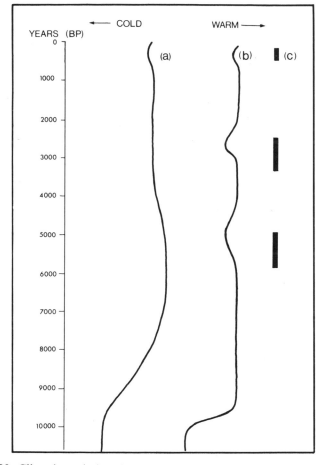

Fig.20. Climatic variation during the Flandrian period. (a) Standard model proposed on the basis of botanical evidence. (b) New model proposed tentatively on the basis of insect evidence. (From Osborne, 1976). (c) Northern Hemisphere glacial maxima. (From Denton and Karlén, 1973)

pointed out that interpretation of insect faunas in climatic terms is based on present-day geographical ranges, and although these are probably more or less reliable, particularly in fairly mobile creatures like insects, there is always the possibility of factors other than climate acting as a control. Laboratory data on thermal tolerances are needed for certain key species before conclusions can be accepted as totally reliable.

In environmental work, insects have been used to demonstrate the increasing impact of man on woodland habitats since Neolithic times. Their main value, however, is in the reconstruction of local environments, since many phytophagous forms are restricted to one species of plant. They are therefore of value in complementing the regional data derived from pollen studies — for example in the investigation of prehistoric trackways. In the case of waterlogged ditches (p.116), insects can give precise information about the species of plant growing alongside the ditch. Dung beetles are often common in archaeological assemblages, demonstrating the former immediate presence of large herbivorous mammals (Osborne, 1969).

Since many species are associated with particular crops or are pests of stored products, the function of archaeological features like pits and buildings can often be determined from insect remains. One species, for example, is a pest in tanneries, and the presence of this and others which thrive on flesh has been taken to indicate the tanning function of a site in medieval York (Buckland, et al., 1974). A particularly elegant example of insect studies is that from a Roman pit at Alcester, Warwickshire (Osborne, 1971). Here it was shown that the pit originally functioned as a 'refuse-pit into which was thrown sweepings from the floor of a leather-goods factory, dung, and general domestic garbage.' Building timbers or furniture were infested with furniture beetles, and the grain stores were infested with a variety of beetle pests, notably the saw-toothed grain beetle, *Oryzaephilus surinamensis*. The surrounding landscape was open meadowland.

Molluscs

Molluscs are of both economic and environmental importance. They are best dealt with on an environmental basis in two groups: (1) Marine and estuarine; (2) Land and freshwater. But a few preliminary comments on the group as a whole are necessary. The part of the animal generally preserved is the shell, and since this is mainly calcium carbonate, the conditions of preservation need to be calcareous. On the whole the information derived from molluscs complements that from plant remains and insects — particularly in providing evidence about the environment of limestone areas. Molluscs too have colonized a wide variety of marine habitats, whereas the insects and plants have not.

Marine and estuarine molluscs (Shackleton, 1969a; Meighan, 1969)

These occur in a variety of coastal deposits — beach sands, cemented gravels, and estuarine clays. Sediments beyond the littoral zone are of little archaeological relevance and have been little studied (but see Norton, 1967). Shells can be extracted very easily by wet sieving, using a $0 \cdot 5$ mm mesh, either in the field or in the laboratory.

There are four main taxonomic groups:

(1) The snails or gastropods. Creatures such as the winkle and whelk; limpets and abalones are also included here.
(2) Bivalves. Creatures with a hinged shell such as the oyster, cockle and mussel.
(3) The scaphopods or elephant-tusk shells. A small group of tusk-shaped shells, much used by early man as ornaments, but of little value in economic or environmental studies.
(4) The cuttlefish. The internal shell or 'bone' of these creatures is often preserved in fragmentary state.

Of these groups, only the first two occur in any abundance in deposits, and they are the main ones used in environmental research.

Ecologically we may recognize sandy shore, rocky shore and estuarine species, and their main value is undoubtedly in providing data about ancient coastal habitats. For example, today in the Swansea Bay area of South Wales there is a sandy beach, at least in the upper shore zone. Sediments immediately beneath the modern sands, however, are of a finer character and contain estuarine and salt-marsh species of mollusc which tolerate lower salinity than occurs on the open shore and which are mud-dwellers (Fig.35). Clearly there have been considerable changes of coastal morphology in the area. Evidence of former shorelines may be preserved as zones of holes made by marine rock-boring species.

Where molluscs have been collected by man for food and the shells accumulated in middens or occupation layers, the composition of the assemblages can indicate the nature of the contemporary coastline and the environments exploited (see p.88 for a further example). It must be borne in mind, however, that variations in relative abundance with time (Fig.21) may be due not only to coastal changes but to a number of factors connected with man — over-exploitation, changes in human food preferences, or in the

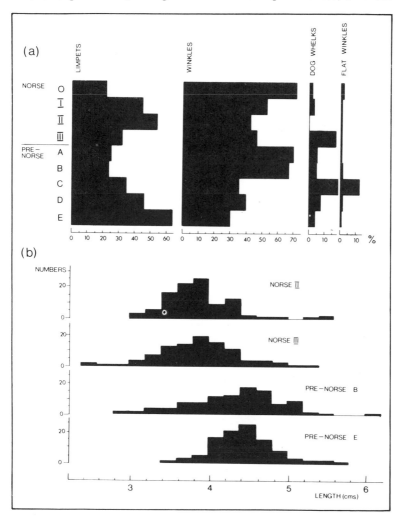

Fig.21. Marine Mollusca (shellfish). (a) Changes in the relative abundance of four species of shellfish in a midden from Buckquoy, Orkney. (b) Distribution curves of limpet length from four selected horizons of the Buckquoy midden. (J. G. Evans, unpublished data from an excavation by Dr Anna Ritchie)

type of economy. Limpets, for example, were favoured in pre-historic Britain, but not so from the Roman period onwards. As with the larger mammals, some marine molluscs are not only indirect indicators of the environment but an integral part of man's environment itself in that they were exploited by him.

In addition to *species diversity*, which we have been discussing so far, other measurements can be made. These include shell *size* and *form*, but as with species diversity, the exact significance of changes through time of these aspects — whether environmental or economic — is not always clear. A decrease in size, for example, may indicate over-exploitation by man or some sort of environmental change (Fig.21). In the example shown it is interesting that as the importance of limpets declines in the Viking period, so too does the average size of the shells being exploited. Likewise with changes of shell form; environmental change or a change in the area being exploited may equally be involved. For example, limpets may be conical, intermediate or flat, depending on whereabouts on the shore they occur — conical forms occurring in the upper shore zone, flat forms close to low water and intermediate forms in the mid-tide zone. Plots of height against length — which is a rough index of form — can show at a glance whether the assemblage is a mixed one or has been collected from a specific area of the shore.

On the whole, marine molluscs have not been found very suitable for climatic interpretation (Norton, 1967). But it is interesting to note that one of the earliest recognitions of the Flandrian thermal maximum was through the study of marine molluscs in sediments exposed in excavations for Belfast harbour (Praeger, 1896). Species were present in the deposits which today are restricted to warmer waters.

Land and freshwater molluscs (Evans, 1972a; Sparks, 1961; 1969)

Freshwater molluscs have been little studied in direct association with archaeological horizons (but see Kerney, 1971), but they have yielded valuable data about changing river and lake regimes in purely Quaternary contexts. They are often extremely prolific in calcareous sediments. Extraction is done by wet-sieving using a mesh size of 0·5 mm, and about 1·0 kg of sediment.

Four ecological groups have been proposed:

(1) Slum species. These occur for example in small bodies of water, poorly aerated and subject to periodic drying.

(2) Catholic species. Found in more or less all types of freshwater habitat except the worst slums.
(3) Ditch species. A group preferring plant-rich, slow streams.
(4) Moving-water species. Species living in large bodies of well-
oxygenated water.

Interpretation is based on these groups and generally provides
information about local aquatic regimes. One archaeological context in which freshwater molluscs are fairly frequent is the ditch, pit
and well category (p.116). Here the molluscan fauna can indicate
whether the site was subject to periodic drying or held standing
water all year round.

In interglacial contexts, exotic species now extinct in Britain and
sometimes of more southerly distribution can yield climatic data
(Sparks, 1957). But due to the buffering effect of the aquatic
environment, freshwater molluscs are not particularly useful as
climatic indicators.

Some freshwater molluscs are of economic value, notably the
larger mussels, and were often collected for food by early man.

Land molluscs — slugs and snails — have been more widely
studied and occur in a whole variety of contexts of more or less
archaeological relevance.

The main ones are as follows:

(1) Buried soils.
(2) Various archaeological sediments infilling ditches, pits and
wells.
(3) Slopewash deposits including ploughwash and solifluxion
debris.
(4) Blown sand and loess.
(5) Tufa and travertine.
(6) Freshwater deposits.

For some reason, probably adverse habitat conditions, land
molluscs are rare in cave deposits.

Extraction is done in the same way as for freshwater shells.
Hydrogen peroxide may be used to aid the breakdown of the sediment.

The results of molluscan analysis are presented in histogram
form in a manner comparable to the pollen diagram (Fig.22).

Interpretation is based on present-day habitat preferences and
geographical ranges, the former being used in local environmental
studies, the latter in climatic work. In Britain, the following
ecological groups are recognized:

(1) Woodland. Species living in generally shaded habitats.
(2) Open-country. Species living in grassland, arable and scree habitats.
(3) Catholic. Species capable of living in a wide variety of habitats.
(4) Marsh. Species living in marshes.

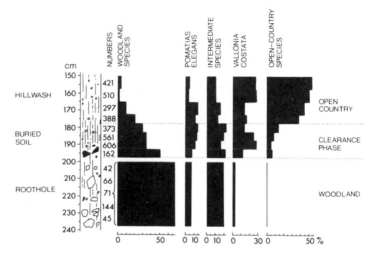

Fig.22. Land-snail histogram. The diagram is from the base of a Flandrian dry-valley fill (p.97) in the Chilterns, Buckinghamshire. It shows the changes from woodland to open-country brought about by prehistoric farmers in the second millennium B.C. The reality of the 'clearance phase' is demonstrated by the *Pomatias elegans* peak. (From Evans, 1972a)

In the Great Plains of North America and also in central Europe, there is a typical *steppe fauna* at certain stages of the Pleistocene (Fig.23). And *cave faunas* contain a few characteristic species. Very few species are restricted to precisely defined habitats, and none to particular species of plant. It is therefore essential that whole faunas are used in habitat reconstruction. Their main value is in interpreting changes in vegetation structure, humidity, soil stability and, in particular, the various effects of man.

Apart from the broad ecological groupings of land molluscs very little quantitative work has been done on modern faunas, and there is still a lot we need to know about certain key species, especially those in the open-country group. In addition there are a number of problems of interpretation related to possible habitat changes in the molluscan species, especially habitats modified by man. For example, some species which lived in woodland during the mid-Flandrian are today *synanthropic*, that is they are closely associated with human habitations, rubbish dumps and so forth. Other species have become greatly restricted due to competition with forms introduced by man in historical times. Present-day habitat preferences are not always a good guide.

A major problem lies in assessing to what extent a subfossil assemblage is a reflection of the fauna — and hence the environment — of an area as a whole and not just the locus from which it came. This applies particularly to the fauna from buried soils; in the case of slopewash deposits which represent the sweepings from a wide area it is not so critical. As yet, little progress has been made on this problem although in practice, where a vertical sequence of faunas is preserved, it is the *relative* differences from one level to the next that give the main clue to the environment, not the *absolute* composition of the fauna. There are two other factors, both of which probably cancel out the effects of very local habitat heterogeneity. One is the fact that a fossil assemblage probably always incorporates several generations; the other is the mobility of the animals. Moreover, work that has been done on modern faunas suggests that ancient assemblages are indeed often reflecting a fairly wide area of countryside.

In Britain, the most important results are those that have a bearing on the ecological history of the chalklands (Fig.22) and the coastal sand-dune areas of the western seaboard (p.86). In parts of central Europe, especially Czechoslovakia, land molluscan analysis constitutes the main technique of Quaternary studies. Deposits of calcareous loess, river gravels and travertine are particularly suitable for preserving shell, and long sequences of environmental history have been recovered (Fig.23). Elsewhere, much less has been done.

Land molluscs can also yield information about ancient climates but they are probably not as useful in this respect as insects. In Britain, present European distribution is used as a guide to climatic tolerances. Again, total assemblages rather than individual species must be used, although certain species are sometimes characteristic of particular zones. For example, the species *Discus ruderatus* is now extinct from Britain but was formerly present in the early Flandrian. Its present central European distribution suggests that it was inhibited by the increase in oceanicity which took place in mid-Flandrian times (the Boreal-Atlantic transition) (Table 5, p.133), and this is supported by the fact that it was replaced at more or less precisely this time by the closely similar species *Discus rotundatus* which has a more westerly distribution in Europe (Table 2, p.101).

Not only climate, but climate change and the direction of change are important in controlling the composition of faunal assemblages. For instance, during an early-glacial period (cooling climate) the fauna was different from that of a late-glacial (warming climate) (Table 4, p.132), *even although the climate itself during the two periods was similar.* In an early-glacial many species persist

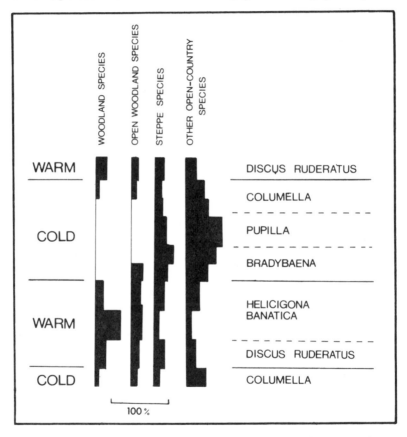

Fig.23. Generalized molluscan histogram from the middle Elbe region, Germany, through two 'glacial' (cold)/'interglacial' (warm) cycles. Only selected ecological groups are shown. On the right some of the species characteristic of each zone are given. Note the presence of different indicators in the early-glacial (*Bradybaena*) and late-glacial (*Columella*) periods. (From Mania, 1973)

which are absent from the subsequent late-glacial (Fig.23). Differing rates of migration and colonization as the climate warmed up were probably responsible for the absence of some species from the late-glacial faunas.

Other invertebrates

There is a whole variety of other invertebrates that may occur on archaeological sites or in situations likely to yield environmental evidence. They are only of lesser importance than the molluscs and the insects in that they do not occur as frequently or have not been so thoroughly studied. The various principles have, on the whole, been covered in considering the animal groups already dealt with. Only special points will therefore be mentioned below.

Foraminifera

Various groups of the great phylum of single-celled animals, the Protozoa, and in particular the Foraminifera, occur in marine and freshwater sediments. There is a variety of forms (Fig.24), and they are preserved by virtue of a calcareous, or in some cases siliceous, skeleton or shell. A sieve size of about 0·1 mm is needed for their extraction. The Foraminifera are good climatic indicators, and in

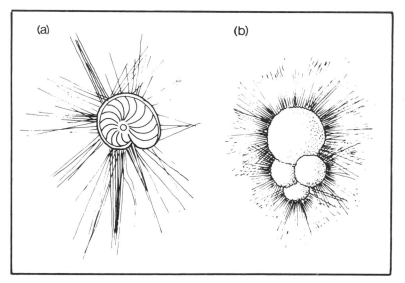

Fig.24. Foraminifera. (a) *Elphidium*. (b) *Globigerina bulloides*. Both × 25.

coastal studies complement the local environmental evidence of the molluscs (Funnell, 1961; Funnell and West, 1962). They are also of importance in deep-sea core work (p.81).

Cladocera and Ostracoda (Frey, 1964)

The Cladocera and Ostracoda are two groups of small bivalve Crustacea — creatures which are related to the crabs, crayfish and so on, but which are often no larger than a pin-head. The animal is enclosed by two valves rather like a miniature mussel (Fig.25). They occur in a variety of aquatic habitats, but their main value is in palaeolimnological work — the study of ancient lake sediments.

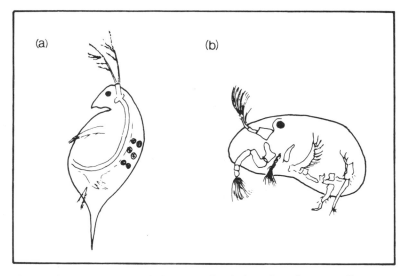

Fig.25. Crustacea. (a) A cladoceran, *Daphnia pulex*, the water flea. (b) An ostracod, *Cypris*. Both × 10.

Cladocera, for example, have been extracted from late Pleistocene deposits in Lake Zeribar, Iran, and have yielded information about the environment at the human cultural transition from hunting to agriculture in this key area (Megard, 1967).

Larger Crustacea

A number of larger Crustacea, mainly crab fragments, and

occasionally goose barnacles, turn up in calcareous coastal middens. They are undoubtedly human food debris. The goose barnacles occur on floating objects in the sea, to which they are attached by a stalk. The more familiar acorn barnacles are sometimes found in middens attached to the shells of various species of mollusc.

Echinoderms

The echinoderms include sea urchins, heart urchins and starfish. They are very infrequent on archaeological sites due to their brittle nature. It is generally only the spines and test (or shell) fragments of sea urchins that are recovered, and then only from coastal middens where, as with the larger Crustacea, they are human food debris. The gonads, or reproductive organs, are considered a delicacy.

Helminths

Various groups of internal parasitic worms, or helminths, have been recorded from a variety of contexts, generally as eggs or cysts. The main groups are the round worms — or nematodes — the flukes and the tapeworms. There are records of both human and animal species (Taylor, 1955; Pike and Biddle, 1966). The contexts include cess pits, coprolites and the preserved stomach contents and other organs of bog burials, mummies and frozen mammoths (Allison, et al., 1974; Vereshchagin, 1975). These have provided to date information largely of a cultural kind — general sanitation of a settlement or community, and the level of infestation of animal and human populations. Plant nematode cysts have also been recovered in a few instances (Webley, 1974).

Coprolites (Callen, 1969; Heizer, 1969)

Coprolites (fossil dung) are best preserved under arid conditions, especially in caves, and have been particularly well studied in the New World. They can be reconstituted by the addition of suitable chemicals such as trisodium phosphate, and various types of plant and animal debris — including the parasites just discussed — extracted. The information yielded is generally of a cultural kind and indicates the various types of food eaten, and also, of course, the environments exploited.

Oxygen isotope analysis (Shackleton, 1969a; 1973)

Oxygen isotope analysis is a method of determining marine palaeo-temperatures from the calcareous shells of organisms such as molluscs and Foraminifera. The principles are quite straight-forward. There are two isotopes of oxygen, 0-16 (the normal form) and 0-18. The ratio of these in the calcium carbonate deposited as shell varies with temperature, but once deposited, remains stable. By measuring the ratio of the two isotopes therefore, using a machine known as a mass spectrometer, an index of water temperature at the time the organism was alive can be obtained.

The technique has two main applications. In deep-sea core work (Fig.33) measurements on Foraminifera have produced sequences of climatic change for a substantial part of the Upper Pleistocene. This evidence tends on the whole to support the ecological evidence of the faunal assemblages themselves. Of more archaeological relevance, oxygen isotope analysis has been applied to marine molluscs from coastal middens in order to ascertain whether these were seasonal or not, and if the former, during which season of the year occupation took place (Fig.26).

Seasonality of occupation

The practice of human communities of exploiting different environments — and possibly leading different life-styles — at different times of the year has its roots well back in the Lower Palaeolithic. It reaches its greatest complexity in the Mesolithic period and in recent groups such as certain North American Indian tribes. Transhumance, already mentioned, is just one aspect of this phenomenon. It will be useful, therefore, to bring together the various methods of determining the season of occupation of a site, particularly as most of them are based on the evidence of animal remains.

(1) The presence of migratory animals such as particular species of bird or fish.
(2) The age range of individuals, particularly if, as with some mammals, there is a specific breeding season.
(3) Otolith ring studies.
(4) The condition of deer antlers — whether attached to the skull or shed (Clark, 1954). Each species of deer sheds its antlers at a particular and fairly precise time of the year, and in some cases the antlers are immediately eaten to replace calcium loss. Shed antlers may therefore be used to indicate

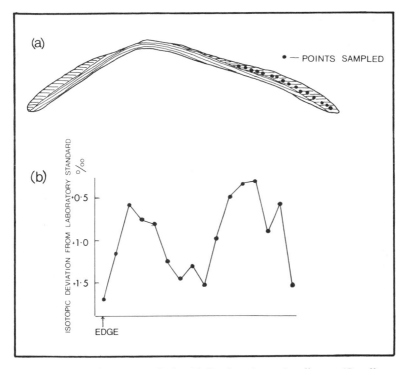

Fig.26. Oxygen isotope analysis. (a) Section through a limpet (*Patella tabularis*) from the southern African coast showing the growth layers and points sampled for analysis. (b) Analysis curve. The shell is a modern one, collected in winter, and the analysis covers just two years' growth. (From Shackleton, 1973)

      when a site was occupied fairly accurately, while unshed or part-grown antlers indicate a range of a few months.

(5) Oxygen isotope analysis of shells can indicate the period of occupation of a midden (Fig.26).

(6) Insect evidence — for example the presence of winged ants which only occur at particular seasons.

(7) The presence of plant parts only produced seasonally — e.g. flowers and seeds.

There are also aspects relating to the general topography of a site that might give a clue to the season of occupation. Some sites, for instance, could logically be seen as being flooded during winter, that is if water-table level were similar to that of today.

4 Soils and sediments

We turn now to a consideration of the soils and sediments from which the various biological remains described in Chapters 2 and 3 derive (Butzer, 1972; Cornwall, 1958; Limbrey, 1975). First of all, the main physical and chemical features used in describing soils and sediments are outlined. (Methods of analysis involving laboratory techniques are not discussed. For these see Cornwall, 1958 and Shackley, 1975.) Various processes of physical weathering are then considered, followed by a description of the main sediment types. Chemical weathering agents and other processes leading to soil formation are then outlined, and the chapter concludes with a description of some of the more important soil types.

Physical features

Particle size. The composition of a sediment in terms of the relative abundance of particle sizes — i.e. its texture — is an important clue to its origin. Gravels, for example, tend to be derived from rapid river flow or strong wave action; clays, on the other hand, are laid down in still-water conditions. There are several schemes of classification, one of which — the British system — is given below.

Clay	0·002 mm or less
Silt	0·002–0·06 mm
Sand	0·06–2·0 mm
Gravel (Pebbles)	2·0–60·0 mm
Stones (Cobbles)	60·0 mm and over

Varying percentages of clay, silt and sand are used to give precision to soil descriptions — e.g. silty clay. A more or less equal mixture of all three is called a *loam*.

The results of particle-size analysis are presented in the form of a cumulative percentage graph (Fig.27) in which the horizontal axis is the particle size (a logarithmic scale is used) and the vertical axis the cumulative percentage. A graph with a gradual slope is generally a loam; one with a steep slope, a well-sorted sediment in which one particle size predominates. The degree of sorting is an important indicator of origin.

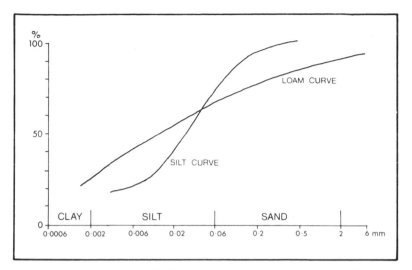

Fig.27. Particle-size analysis. Specimen curves of a loam and a silt. (From Cornwall, 1953)

Particle shape. The two main shapes are rounded and angular. Rounded particles indicate a substantial period of transport, either by stream, wind or wave action. Angular particles indicate little or no transport and are mainly found in scree and solifluxion debris. Intermediate shapes are known as sub-angular and sub-rounded.

Grain surface. Features of the surface of sand grains can indicate whether the material is of wind-blown or aquatic origin. Under the low-power microscope, wind-blown grains have mat or dulled surfaces, grains deposited in fluviatile or marine environments are glossy and polished. Other diagnostic surface features can be observed under the scanning electron microscope.

Gross morphology. Other features such as the position of a deposit in relation to topography, and the degree of layering or bedding, can provide clues to its environment of deposition. Lake sediments for example are often finely bedded; glacial deposits, on the other hand, typically show no trace of bedding at all (Fig.45).

Chemical features

Mineral composition. Determination of the mineral composition of soils and sediments is done microscopically, generally using a polarizing microscope. In this, the light is transmitted in one plane, giving better characterization to the various minerals than does the ordinary light microscope (Read, 1962). Thin sections for examination are prepared by consolidating the soil or sediment with resin and grinding a smooth, flat surface; this surface is fixed to a microscope slide and the other surface then ground down until the section becomes transparent. This technique can also be applied to rocks, which do not of course need consolidating.

Mineral composition yields data on three important aspects:

(1) The degree of weathering in a soil.
(2) The source of rocks in far-travelled deposits such as boulder clay.
(3) The source of raw materials collected by man for pottery and stone implement manufacture.

The breakdown of minerals in the parent rock, leading ultimately to the formation of soil, takes place in a number of stages. The mineral composition, therefore, will give information on the degree of weathering, and this in turn may have climatic implications.

In the study of glacial deposits that may be far-travelled, erratic rocks, particularly if of igneous origin, can often be traced to specific outcrops many hundreds of kilometres away. In this way, the source and direction of ice movement can be reconstructed.

In the study of artefacts derived from inorganic raw materials — particularly clay and stone (p.6) — it is again the provenance of the raw materials that is of interest. This can tell us not only what environments were being exploited but also something about possible cultural contacts. The best known example is the tracing of the Stonehenge bluestones to the Prescelly Mountains in Dyfed, but the technique has been widely applied to pottery (e.g. Williams and Jenkins, 1976) and Neolithic stone axes (Evans, *et al.*, 1962).

Other techniques of mineralogical analysis have been developed for studying trace elements, particularly suitable for rocks like flint and obsidian which do not have large-scale variations of mineral composition and crystalline structure (e.g. Hallam, *et al.*, 1976).

Humus content. Analysis of the humus content of a soil or sediment is useful for detecting buried soil surfaces if these are not otherwise apparent. Humus is decomposed organic matter combined with a mineral component, and is generally concentrated at the soil surface and in the upper layers.

Phosphate content. Phosphate derives from decomposed dung or bone — ' . . . the concentration of livestock on part of an inhabited site, or the day-to-day occupation of a restricted area . . . may increase the accumulation of phosphorus-rich wastes . . . ' (Proudfoot, 1976). The most familiar examples are the accumulation of bird guano on various Pacific islands and the buildup of bird and bat guano in caves.

Phosphate analysis has three main archaeological applications:

(1) The location of settlement sites and the mapping of their extent.
(2) The identification of occupation horizons in archaeological deposits.
(3) The identification of the former presence of bone in pits.

The last two applications are especially relevant in acid soils where bone is usually destroyed. Phosphate analysis may also be used to determine whether a soil is natural or has been formed largely by the artificial buildup of manure and other occupation debris — 'plaggen soils'.

Colour. Soil colour is a useful guide to humus and iron content. Dark-browns, greys or black usually indicate high humus content, and thus an old topsoil. Paler colours indicate either rapid deposition of sediments or leaching in a soil. Orange and red colours indicate high iron content, which in turn may be an indication of podsolization (p.77). Colour is usually defined by a formula — e.g. 7·5YR 3/4 — by matching the soil sample with a standard, the Munsell Colour Chart being the most widely used set of standards. Three variables, hue, value and chroma, are used. In the example quoted, hue is 7·5YR, the colour in relation to red, yellow, etc. The value is 3/, and this is the lightness of the colour. /4 refers to the chroma and this is defined as the strength of the colour. Descriptive names are attached to each formula, 7·5YR 3/4 being 'dark brown', a familiar soil colour in the British Isles. It is important that standard colours are used in soil and sediment description to enable comparison to be made from site to site.

pH. This is a measure of the acidity/alkalinity of a soil, and is an important guide to the types of biological indicator that might be expected to survive. The scale ranges from 0 to 14. pH 7 is neutral, less than 7 is acid and above 7 is alkaline or basic. On the whole soils and sediments range from pH 3·5 — very acid peats — to pH 8·5 — highly alkaline soils on chalk. Extreme values above 8·5 are recorded for sodium soils, and at the other end of the scale values below 3·0 are not unusual.

Physical weathering and sedimentation

The soils and sediments met with in archaeological and environmental work are the products of various types of weathering and/or sedimentation. There are two sorts of weathering — chemical and physical. Physical weathering categories are as follows:

> *Insolation.* Alternating heat and cold on a diurnal or annual basis causes fragments to break off a rock surface.
> *Frost action.* Cracks in a rock surface are enlarged by freezing water; eventually rock chips are removed.
> *Wind action.* Fine particles carried by wind erode rock surfaces.
> *Wave/river action.* Pebbles and other particles carried by waves/rivers erode coastlines and valleys.
> *Glaciers.* Pebbles and boulders in an ice sheet, and the ice itself, erode the rock surface over which it passes.
> *Solifluxion.* Solifluxion debris erodes the surface over which it passes.
> *Man.* Tillage and overgrazing by man's animals are important factors in causing soil erosion.

The products of physical weathering are subjected to varying degrees of transport and are ultimately laid down as *sediments* (Fig.28). These may continue to be subjected to minor physical weathering, and also to chemical weathering; this ultimately leads to the formation of *soil*. Before describing these chemical processes and the soils that result from them we must first deal briefly with the various sediment types.

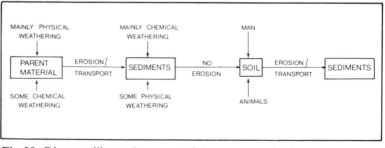

Fig.28. Diagram illustrating some of the processes in the weathering/erosion/sedimentation cycle.

Types of sediment

Sediments can be classified in various ways. Ideally we should adopt a classification which uses particle size as a basis — various types of sand, silt and so forth — but in practice an environmental classification is more realistic. Three broad groups can be recognized: aquatic, terrestrial (or subaerial) and aeolian.

Aquatic sediments. These group conveniently into marine, estuarine and freshwater. *Gravels* consist of well-rounded particles and are formed in 'high-energy' situations — the upper shoreline, where they may occur as prominent storm beaches, and in fast-flowing rivers. Consolidated gravels are known as *conglomerate.* Finer aquatic sediments occur lower down the shoreline — where there is a gradation from *coarse sand* to *mud* — and in gently flowing rivers. The finest muds and clays occur in backwaters, lakes, estuaries and deep-sea basins.

Sorting in aquatic sediments can be more clearly defined by mechanical analysis, and reflects the simplicity/complexity of the sedimentation processes. For example, sand laid down in a river-beach or open-shore situation would show a steep curve. If, at a later stage, it were subjected to slopewashing or chemical weathering in a terrestrial environment — during for example a period of low sea level — it would show a gentler slope.

The distinction between sand of an aquatic origin and sand of an aeolian origin has already been discussed (p.65).

Terrestrial sediments. There is a greater variety of processes involved in the formation of terrestrial sediments. Five main groups are recognized:

(1) Slopewash deposits.
(2) Cave deposits.
(3) Precipitates.
(4) Organic sediments.
(5) Glacial deposits.

(1) *Slopewash deposits.* Where drainage is impeded on slopes — even of as little as $2°$ — soil and rock rubble may be moved downhill. *Solifluxion debris* forms under cold-climate conditions, generally in the periglacial zone (p.95). Rapid thawing of frozen ground in spring causes the sudden release of quantities of water

which, because of the permanently frozen nature of the subsoil, cannot drain away. It therefore flows downhill taking soil and rock debris with it. Solifluxion — literally 'soil flow' — does not, however, necessarily require permafrost. One cause is simply the continuous freeze-thaw cycle at the surface layers which maintains their instability. On the mountains of the Welsh and Scottish uplands, solifluxion lobes are still forming. Solifluxion deposits may be coarse and unbedded or finely bedded, almost water-lain in appearance. Some of the most spectacular results of periglacial solifluxion can be seen in the sarsen and other rock streams of the North Wiltshire Downs, Dartmoor and the Prescelly Mountains.

The other main type of slopewash deposit is called *ploughwash*. It is generally formed as a result of man's activities. Breaking up of the soil by tillage or animal overgrazing causes loss of structure, breakdown of soil crumbs, and clogging of the pores so vital for drainage. As with solifluxion, drainage is impeded and, with the lack of vegetation cover to hold the soil together, hillwashing ensues.

Hillwash and solifluxion deposits are characterized by poor sorting and gentle particle-size analysis curves. The particles are angular to sub-rounded, rarely rounded.

Scree can be included in this section although not really forming in the same way. Scree forms simply by rock fragments being detached by insolation and frost-weathering from a cliff and accumulating at its base through gravity. The particles are always angular. Scree often becomes consolidated in a calcite matrix and is then known as *breccia*.

(2) *Cave deposits*. A whole variety of deposits form in caves, a few peculiar to the caves themselves, others more typical of normal terrestrial situations (p.100). Stalagmite and breccia are characteristic, but *cave earth* is probably the only unique sediment type. The term cave earth is generally applied to any loamy or organic sediment which cannot otherwise be more exactly classified. In effect cave earth consists of a complex of animal and human occupation debris, decayed bone, faeces and so on, as well as material derived by slow mechanical weathering of the cave roof and walls, and wind-blown material brought in from outside. The reason for the accumulation of this material in caves is that the normal processes of chemical weathering and soil formation which lead to the total breakdown of organic material in the open air do not take place as rapidly. Dryness is a contributory factor. This is especially so in some Great Basin caves in western North America where coprolites, plant remains and other organic debris such as feathers may all be preserved (Heizer, 1969). The attraction of

caves for shelter and occupation, as well as the fact that they are natural catchment situations anyway, makes the buildup of thick deposits of cave earth inevitable. In fissures, animal bone debris often constitutes an important part of the fill since fissures, where they open onto the surface, provide foci for carnivore and hominid activity, as well as acting as natural pitfall traps.

(3) *Precipitates*. The main types of precipitate with which we are concerned in the temperate regions of the world are calcareous — calcium carbonate. In tropical regions (p.80) silica becomes mobile and precipitates out as *silcrete*, and in inland basins strong evaporation leads to the formation of *saltpans*.

The two main types of calcareous precipitate are *tufa* and *stalagmite*, and they form in more or less the same way. Water, charged with lime in solution, breaks out at the surface and evaporates leaving a precipitate of calcium carbonate. In caves the process of evaporation is slow due to the enclosed, humid environment, and the resulting precipitate is often hard. It is then known as stalagmite. It may form as layers or crusts on the cave floor sealing earlier sediments, or it may form as spectacular and beautiful stalagmites and stalactites.

In open-air situations, ground water coming to the surface in swampy or marshy environments tends to evaporate more quickly than in caves. The resulting precipitate is then known as tufa, a soft, sometimes compact and almost cheese-like, deposit. Molluscan and radiocarbon evidence (p.99) indicate that most tufas formed during periods of warm humid climate during the thermal maximum of an interglacial or the Flandrian period, and in a local environment of tree-shaded swamp.

Algal marl is an organic precipitate, similar in appearance to tufa, but formed in freshwater by the precipitation of calcium carbonate aided by the biological activities of Algae. The distinction between algal marl and tufa is not always clear, and cases of difficulty must be resolved by molluscan analysis.

(4) *Organic sediments*. In this category the main sediment is *peat*. Peats can be classified quite simply on the basis of their contained plant remains. The main types are (a) *Sphagnum* peat which forms in fairly acid conditions and which, in addition to the moss, *Sphagnum*, may contain varying amounts of heather and cotton grass; (b) brushwood peat which forms under carr conditions — for example alder woodland; and (c) reedswamp peat which is essentially an aquatic deposit made up of the stems and leaves of the reed, *Phragmites*. Peats are essentially pure organic deposits formed under completely anaerobic conditions in which the activities of micro-organisms in breaking down organic matter are

totally inhibited. In some cases, peat has been subjected to partial breakdown in which all macroscopic plant remains are destroyed but in which the essentially organic nature of the deposit is still apparent. This is known as amorphous peat. (For further discussion see p.107.)

(5) *Glacial deposits*. The main glacial deposit is *till* or *boulder clay*. This material is formed by glacial erosion of rock and consists of a very ill-sorted mixture of boulders and smaller pebbles in a matrix of finer material. The stones are all of different sizes and are generally of a variety of types and origins. Completely rounded stones are rare — most are sub-rounded or sub-angular. Analysis of the various rock types in a till can give some indication of their source (p.66), and a study of stone orientation can indicate the direction of ice movement.

Immediately beyond the edge of a glacier, *outwash sands and gravels* usually occur. These show crude bedding and poor sorting.

Aeolian sediments. The main characteristic of aeolian or wind-blown sediments is that they are finely sorted, showing steep mechanical analysis curves (Fig.27). The two main types are wind-blown sand or *coversand* and wind-blown silt or *loess*.

Coversands form by a process called *saltation*. The wind picks up sand grains in a gust — generally from the sea-shore or from pro-glacial outwash deposits — and deposits them as soon as the gust subsides. A subsequent gust may transport them further inland or away from the ice front. In this manner, the sand is blown in stages and may be transported several kilometres from source. Coversands sometimes become consolidated and are then known as *sand rock*.

The main episodes of coversand formation were (a) in the Last Glaciation when there were several periods (Fig.34), and (b) in the Flandrian when many coastal coversand deposits formed intermittently from Neolithic times onwards (p.86).

Loess is formed in a different manner. Silt particles are sufficiently fine to be transported considerable distances by wind, irrespective of strong gusts. In the high pressure regions that build up over an ice sheet, winds radiate outwards transporting silt particles many hundreds of kilometres before their carrying power subsides and the silt is deposited. Most loess deposits — at any rate in northwest and central Europe and in North America — are of periglacial origin. But there is another reason for the concentration of silt-size material peripheral to an ice sheet. Physical weathering of rock by insolation and frost shattering cannot proceed beyond the silt size — the particles are too small for these processes to act further.

There is therefore an accumulation of silt-size material even before wind-sorting begins to operate. (See also p.95.)

Volcanic deposits. Volcanic deposits constitute a separate category since a variety of processes and environments of deposition are involved. Some, such as lava flows, are terrestrial. Others, such as deposits of volcanic ash, are aeolian. Yet others, in being laid down in lacustrine or marine environments, are, at least in part, of aquatic origin.

Chemical weathering processes and the formation of soil

We have discussed briefly the ways in which rocks are broken down by processes of physical weathering, and how the material is transported and sedimented (Fig.28). It is now necessary to describe the processes which act upon these sediments to convert them into soil (Russell, 1961).

Rainwater is not pure but is a weak solution of *carbonic acid*, formed by the solution of carbon dioxide from the atmosphere. Carbonic acid breaks down some of the minerals in a sediment, particularly calcium carbonate. *Nitric acid*, formed by lightning, is another, although more intermittent, chemical weathering agent. Plants — both decaying and alive — also liberate acids, the most important being *humic acid* — a complex organic compound whose molecular structure is not fully understood. All these acids bring about the solution and breakdown of various mineral components in the parent material which may then be lost into the ground-water by *leaching* (Fig.31). Precipitation of dissolved chemicals from ground-water gives rise to a variety of deposits such as iron pans and silcretes, as well as the tufas and stalagmites already described.

An important aspect of soil formation is the creation of the *clay minerals* (Limbrey, 1975). The chemistry and physical properties of these fascinating substances is totally beyond the scope of this book, but a few general comments can be made. The clay minerals are formed by the breakdown and alteration of the parent material by the action of the various acids mentioned above and simply by the action of water — a process known as *hydrolysis*. They are important in being the seat for many of the elements necessary for plant growth, and in providing the framework for the complex chemical reactions that take place in the soil. Their very small size gives them certain physical properties, particularly the ability to bond together in loose chemical associations, and it is largely due to the clay minerals that the physical structure and stability of the soil are maintained.

The breakdown of organic matter yields a finely-divided, amorphous material which combines with the organic fraction to form *humus*. Humus too, like the clay minerals, is involved in maintaining the physical and chemical equilibrium of soil. Both materials are combined around a lattice of the larger silt- and sand-size particles to form *soil crumbs*. These constitute an open mesh of organic and inorganic material, the spaces of which are filled with the *soil solution*. They are vital for the maintenance of soil chemistry and fertility, as well as free drainage. Breakdown of the crumb structure is the first stage of soil degradation.

The *soil* can thus be defined as the result of chemical and physical weathering acting upon the parent material to form a medium which can support plant growth.

The various weathering and soil processes described — leaching, formation of humus, release of clay minerals, reprecipitation of leached chemicals — lead to the phenomenon of *horizonation* in the soil. A section through a soil shows a number of horizons which are not layers in the stratigraphical sense but the result of processes operating within the soil. The sequence of horizons is known as the *soil profile*. There are a number of systems of classification, some of which are complex. The following is a useful summary:

Horizon	Characteristics
A	Upper, humus horizons.
E	Horizons from which mineral and organic matter has been lost by leaching or *eluviation*.
B	Horizons of accumulation or *illuviation*.
(B)	Horizons of chemical weathering below the A-horizon, but lacking illuviation (pronounced B-bracket).
C	The parent material.

Various suffixes can be used for clearer definition. For example, Bh is a horizon of humus illuviation. The E-horizons are sometimes referred to as A_2-horizons.

The main soil types (Cornwall, 1958; Kubiena, 1953; Limbrey, 1975)

There are several soil types which are of importance in environmental archaeology and whose characters provide important information pertaining to past environments, in particular in the study of two aspects — past climates, and the impact of man on the landscape.

Rendsinas (Evans, 1972a). The rendsina is the common soil type of chalk and limestone rocks and calcareous blown sand in north-west Europe. It consists simply of an A-horizon of rich humic material, generally black, overlying the highly calcareous C-horizon (Fig.29).

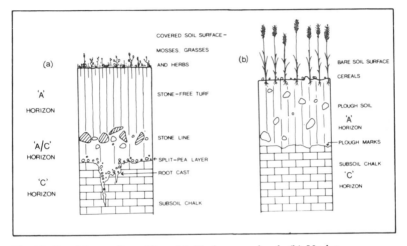

Fig.29. Rendsina soil profiles. (a) Under grassland. (b) Under cultivation.

The reason for the absence of an E- or B-horizon is that the calcium carbonate content is maintained by proximity to, and replacement from, the subsoil. Faunal activity is exceptionally high and probably helps to cycle calcareous matter through the soil. The main organisms are earthworms and mites; larger creatures such as moles and various burrowing rodents are important locally.

Earthworm activity is an important agency in the burial of stones and the production of a *turf line* (Fig.29a). The species involved eject their casts onto the surface of the ground. Collapse of old burrows takes place, and the two processes — surface casting and burrow collapse — cause the gradual downward movement of any material in the soil too large to pass through an earthworm's gut (approximately 2·0 mm). The buried stones come to lie at the base of the turf line as a *stone line*. This process only takes place under the absence of other mechanical disturbance, and the turf line and stone line features in a soil are therefore a good criterion of the absence of tillage (Fig.29a). Conversely, cultivated soils always show a total mixing of stones throughout the A-horizon, and ploughmarks may be visible at the base (Fig.29b).

Another feature of fossil rendsinas — and indeed of other soil types — are hollows at the base of the soil, penetrating the subsoil and filled with organic material. These are generally interpreted as the casts of old tree roots, and are thus an index of former woodland.

The rendsina has been described first because it is the least mature of the various soils that we will consider.

Brownearths. The brownearth forms on subsoils with a pH of around $5 \cdot 5$ to $7 \cdot 5$; they are more or less neutral to slightly acid. In addition to the humic A-horizon they are characterized by a (B)-horizon in which minerals — mainly iron oxides — are released by weathering processes (Fig.30a) but in which there is no accumulation of leached material from above.

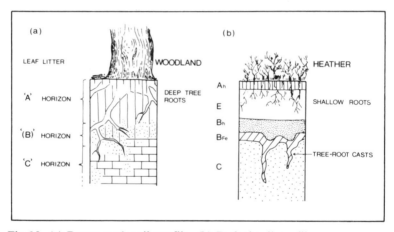

Fig.30. (a) Brownearth soil profile. (b) Podsol soil profile.

Brownearths are characteristic of mixed deciduous woodland which serves to maintain their high base status, their structure and their drainage. Microclimatic variation at the soil surface — involving alternate wetting and drying, and leading to the partial breakdown of the crumb structure — is prevented by the woodland cover. Moreover, chemicals lost by leaching are brought up from the subsoil in the root system of the trees and replaced into the soil in the leaf fall (Fig.31). Drainage is maintained by transpiration of water from the leaves of the forest canopy. These three processes — the maintenance of microclimatic stability, the recycling of chemicals and the transpiration of water — are vital to soil stability. Their disruption — for example by forest clearance — leads to various processes of soil degradation, and in particular to the formation of podsols, sols lessivés and gleys, which we shall now describe.

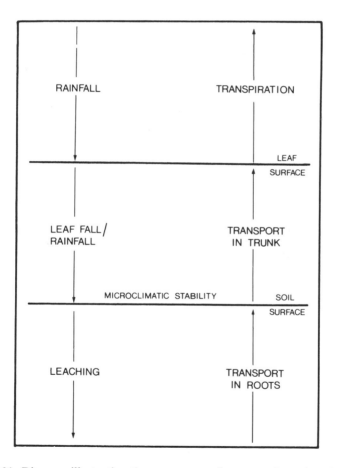

Fig.31. Diagram illustrating the movement of water and nutrients in a woodland soil.

Podsols (Dimbleby, 1962). On very acid subsoils and in areas of high rainfall, the podsol forms. This shows marked leaching effects in having a pronounced E-horizon of ash-grey colour due to the removal of iron and humus, and a pronounced B-horizon in which the iron and humus accumulate, sometimes as a hardpan (Fig.30b). The B-horizon is generally black or deep orange.

The podsol is characteristic of heaths and moorlands, but as shown by the study of buried soils under Neolithic and Bronze Age sites, these areas formerly supported circumneutral brownearths. Modern podsols, too, sometimes show a turf line and stone line. This is a relic feature of former brownearth status, since the surface-casting worms responsible for these features cannot exist in the very low pH of podsols. Tree-root casts are also a prominent feature of many heathland podsols, evidence of former woodland amply supported by pollen analysis. Podsolization is almost certainly due, in some cases, to deforestation.

Sols lessivés. The sol lessivé is a type of brownearth in which clay particles rather than chemical solutions are washed down through the soil and deposited at a lower level as a noticeably clayey Bt-horizon (t=textural). As with the podsol, this type of soil is thought to be a result of human interference with the natural forest vegetation. Stripping of woodland exposes the soil surface to great contrasts of temperature and humidity which tend to break down the crumb structure releasing individual clay particles. These move down through the soil converting the (B)-horizon of a brownearth into the Bt-horizon of a sol lessivé. Again, there is evidence from buried soils in archaeological contexts that these changes have taken place at various times in the past (Limbrey, 1975).

Gleys. Gley soils are waterlogged soils in which the B-horizon is either totally grey, due to the anaerobic conditions of the iron compounds, or grey/orange mottled, due to areas — often around root-holes and cracks — of aerobic conditions in which the iron compounds are orange.

Gleys form in a variety of situations, valley and upland. They have not been much studied archaeologically but one suspects many of them to be of relatively recent origin, having formed through disturbance of the hydrological regime by man — particularly the changes wrought by forest clearance and land exploitation for farming. Pollen analytical studies of Welsh upland gleys (Crampton and Webley, 1964) have demonstrated an early woodland phase (Fig.5).

Chernozems. The chernozems occur mainly on loess in central and eastern Europe, and east into Russia. They are characteristic of more continental climates than obtain in Britain. The main feature of the chernozem is a deep, richly humic A-horizon — up to a metre thick — resting directly on the parent material. Calcium carbonate is removed by leaching and deposited as a crust at the soil base, but there is no development of a true E- or B- horizon, and few nutrients are lost to the ground-water. One of the reasons for the extreme thickness of the humus horizon is that microbial activity is reduced due to the dry climate and extreme low temperatures of the continental winter.

Mediterranean soils. The characteristic Mediterranean soil is the terra rossa. This tends to show a bright red B-horizon due to extreme dehydration of iron compounds in the dry season. There may also be clay illuviation as a Bt-horizon due to strongly seasonal wetting and drying of the soil. However, these features — particularly the bright coloration — may be relics of former, much hotter climate, perhaps during previous interglacials or even the Tertiary period. Unlike the situation in north-west Europe there have been no glaciations in the Mediterranean region (except locally on high mountains) to remove these earlier traces of intense chemical weathering.

Red soils have been found in early Pleistocene deposits in Britain

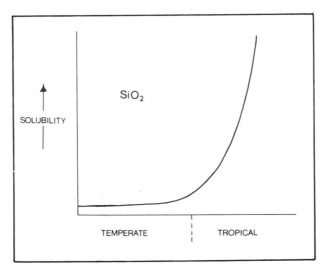

Fig.32. Solubility of silica (SiO_2) under different climatic conditions.

and other temperate regions and are possibly indicative of former sub-tropical climates. But one must be cautious of confusing these with red iron compounds released from parent rocks which may have formed many millions of years ago in the geological past.

Rendsinas of relatively recent origin also occur in Mediterranean countries where the older soils have been lost by erosion.

Tropical soils. Under tropical conditions different weathering processes take place. Silica, which in temperate climates is virtually stable, becomes soluble (Fig.32). The soils, therefore, instead of having silica as their skeletal structure, have iron and aluminium compounds. The commonest tropical soil is the *laterite.* The leached silica may be redeposited elsewhere by evaporation as a cemented crust of *silcrete.*

A characteristic soil of both tropical and mediterranean climates is the *vertisol.* This is a clay soil which forms in lowlying areas on fine-grained sediments, often recent flood loams (Limbrey, 1975). Because of the very clayey nature of the soils and the fact that they occur in areas of strongly seasonal climate, alternate wetting and drying leads to a continual swelling and shrinking of the soil, a process which may be powerful enough to disrupt man-made structures such as paving and fences.

Termites are a feature of tropical soils, important in determining soil fertility and the character of the vegetation. The mounds of these creatures are made of subsoil material and are thus important in counteracting the effects of leaching; termite earth is often spread over areas to prepare ground for cultivation (Limbrey, 1975). In 'termite mound savanna' the mounds may support a different vegetation from that of the surrounding area, especially in poorly-drained soils.

5 Natural situations

The rest of this book is devoted to a variety of environmental situations in which the various indicators discussed in the previous three chapters are likely to occur. There is a convenient, although somewhat artificial, distinction that can be made between natural situations — described in this chapter — and archaeological situations — described in Chapter 6. Cutting across this division there are two major types of situation — (a) buried soils, and (b) sediment catchments.

Buried soils are samples of ancient land surfaces which occur under various archaeological monuments such as barrows, ramparts and so forth, and at the base of, and within, sediments like peat and loess. They are important in providing climatic and environmental information about the past, and are in some ways more reliable in this respect than sediments, since they reflect the normal land surface and environment, not the special environments of deposition. But there are considerable problems in the interpretation of ancient soil profiles — the separation of climatic and environmental factors, the estimation of the time scale, the detection of relic soils, and the possibility that even the soil is not totally representative of a whole area.

Two general points which are applicable to practically all sediment catchment situations can be made:

(1) They are all associated with the accumulation of deep layers of sediment and are thus of value in preserving long records of environmental and archaeological history.
(2) The variation in the environment, often induced by the accumulation of the deposits themselves or the differential infilling of associated features, provides a strong attraction to man.

There is therefore a dual reason for concentrating the efforts of environmental archaeology on such situations.

Offshore sediments and deep-sea cores

Marine sediments may be (a) coastal and (b) offshore and deep-sea.

We begin with the latter because, although of no direct archaeological relevance, it has become apparent in recent years that
they, of all sediment types, are capable of providing a full and
fundamental record of Pleistocene chronology and climate change.

Around the southern basin of the North Sea, sediments of great
depth occur. These have been particularly well studied in Holland,
where they have yielded information about the environmental
changes at the Tertiary/Quaternary transition. In East Anglia,
corings and pollen analysis through shelly sediments known as
'crags' have revealed a sequence of early Pleistocene cold and warm
phases preceding the true glacial/interglacial series (West, 1961;
1968). Work is also being done on deep marine sediments in the
Irish Sea and in the more northerly sectors of the North Sea, in the
latter case associated with the drilling for oil and gas. Cores
brought up have revealed hundreds of metres of Pleistocene sediment, although not all of it marine.

Environmental and climatic data can also be derived from *deep-
sea* cores (Rosholt, *et al.*, 1961) in which the study of small marine
organisms, mainly Foraminifera, gives an indication of temperature change. The relative abundance of particular species varies
with sea temperature, so that by analysing the sediments some
indication of the temperature of deposition can be obtained.
Oxygen isotope analysis can also be applied. The importance of
deep-sea sediments is enhanced in that they can be dated by various
techniques of radioactive assay, and so, although devoid of
archaeological material, they can be used to complement the much
sparser continental record (Fig.33). The most important results
have been in the clarification of the sequence between the Hoxnian
(Holstein) and the Last Glaciation where it now seems there were
more cold/warm oscillations of glacial/interglacial magnitude than
had previously been suspected (Shackleton, 1969b).

Coastlines (Gresswell, 1957; West, 1968)

Ancient coastlines are preserved as a result of either tectonic uplift
(earth movement) or sea-level fall, and both processes may be
closely linked to the effects of glaciation and deglaciation.

Tectonic uplift when specifically linked to the effects of deglaciation is known as *isostatic recovery*. The loss of weight resulting
from the melting of an ice sheet causes land to rise; coastlines are
lifted beyond the influence of the sea and preserved. Good
examples can be seen around the east and south-east coasts of Scotland. In Scandinavia the centre point of recovery after the Last

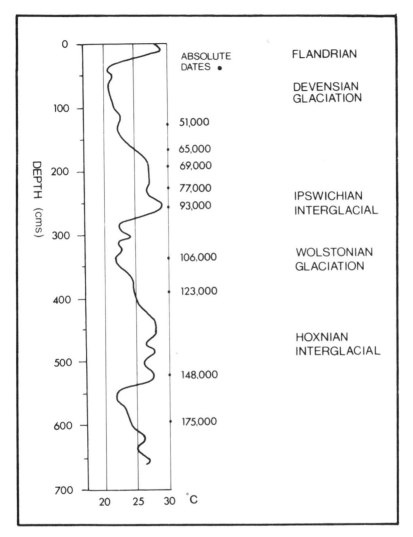

Fig.33. Diagram illustrating deep-sea core work. Isotopic temperature curve from a Caribbean core; absolute dates obtained by measuring the ratio of the isotopes Palladium-231 and Thorium-230. Tentative correlation with the British Pleistocene system on the right. (From Rosholt, *et al.*, 1961)

Glaciation was the head of the Gulf of Bothnia, where the highest Flandrian shoreline is at 295 m above sea-level and where a rate of one centimetre per year is still recorded. These figures give some idea of the magnitude of the process (Clark, 1975).

Isostatic shoreline features are found in areas where former glaciation was pronounced. They vary in height depending on the distance from the greatest thickness of ice — in Scotland the highest Flandrian shoreline is at 15 m, the lowest close to sea-level. Often the beach deposits, because of their suitability for cultivation, were settled by farming communities. Some idea of the land gains involved may be had when it is considered that practically all Finland was submerged at the beginning of the Flandrian. Other features, like caves, were occupied by man, and there are particularly clear examples of these associations in Scotland and southern Scandinavia.

Preservation of the other main type of raised coastal feature is due to the fact that there has been a gradual world-wide — or *eustatic* — lowering of sea-level during the Pleistocene. Former interglacial high sea-levels are not attained in a subsequent interglacial. One of the highest, reflecting an early Pleistocene high sea-level, is recorded at about 200 m and may be seen on the plateau areas of the North Downs, south of London, as spreads of sand and gravel. The most recent, belonging to the Last Interglacial, is widely preserved in various parts of the world at about 8 to 10 m above present sea-level. As with the isostatic shorelines, old sea caves are often associated and these may preserve the remains of human occupation (Fig.34). A typical succession comprises Last Interglacial beach deposits resting on a wave-cut bench and overlain by cold-climate deposits — breccia and coversand — of Last Glaciation age. Classic examples are to be seen in the Gower Peninsula of south Wales (Bowen, 1973); the Mediterranean; and southern Africa (Tankard and Schweitzer, 1976).

Outside the area of isostatic recovery, deposits laid down during the Flandrian or earlier interglacial marine transgressions may be preserved, generally in shallow basins or estuaries (Jelgersma, 1966). These consist of estuarine clays, land surfaces (generally of salt-marsh type) and peat beds (Fig.35). Archaeological material is frequently associated. Study methods consist, on the whole, of augering, pollen, diatom and molluscan analysis; insect remains occur in the peat beds. In some cases the spectacular remains of vertebrates — wild ox, red deer antlers, and whale skeletons — are recovered. Peat beds with tree stools *in situ* may be exposed at low tide as 'submerged forests'. Typical areas where sediments of this type belonging to the Flandrian have been laid down are Swansea Bay and the Somerset Levels on either side of the Bristol Channel,

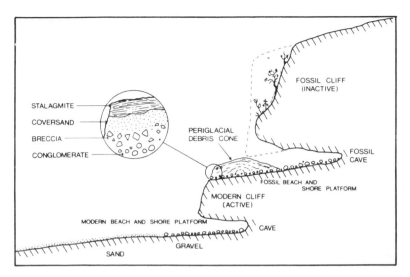

Fig.34. Diagrammatic section through a coastal sea cave and an earlier fossil cave. The area outlined by the dashed line was eroded by periglacial activity and contributed to the debris cone.

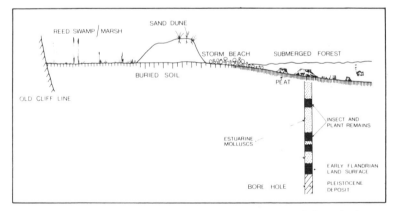

Fig.35. Diagrammatic section through Flandrian coastal deposits in a submerged forest area. In the bore hole, peat is shown black, estuarine clays stippled. The sediments reflect a change from alternating estuarine and peat/forest environments, through a sandy shore and the formation of dunes, to the present storm beach environment.

and thicknesses of 20 m or more are recorded (Godwin, 1940).

We can now summarize the situations in which ancient marine sediments are likely to be preserved:

(1) Below sea-level.
    (a) Offshore and deep-sea Pleistocene sediments.
    (b) Interglacial and Flandrian estuarine deposits.
(2) Isostatic coastline.
    (a) Late-glacial and Flandrian coastal sediments.
    (b) Caves.
(3) Eustatic coastline.
    (a) Interglacial and glacial sediments.
    (b) Caves.

Coastal blown sand

Deposits of blown sand form in any area where there is (a) a supply of sand, (b) an absence of surface vegetation, and (c) at least temporary dryness. If all these conditions are satisfied, wind will pick up dry sand from a bare surface, transport it a short distance, and deposit it. Dunes are formed where the sand collects around any obstacle in its path, such as vegetation or a fence. On the whole in north-west Europe, most deposits of blown sand are coastal, although fossil dunes and coversands of late-glacial age occur in Lincolnshire, the Low Countries and north-west Germany. These sometimes contain organic horizons, which in Holland yield Upper Palaeolithic artefacts and show widespread burning. Here, however, it is the coastal dune systems that are our concern.

Sand-dunes and deposits of blown sand form in coastal areas where there is a broad shallow coastal zone — a bay — on which sand accumulates and is then blown inland. Deposits of blown sand have been recorded over 3 km from the contemporary coastline, and over 100 m above sea-level. A number of environmental zones of archaeological importance may be recognized in a dune system (Fig.36).

(1) The foredunes.
(2) Dune slacks, or pools, behind the foredunes.
(3) Stabilized dunes and sand peripheral to the slacks and fore-dunes.

Sand dunes thus create variability in the environment — active dune surfaces, stable grassland, and slacks with reed-swamp, marsh and open water — which enhances the suitability of the area

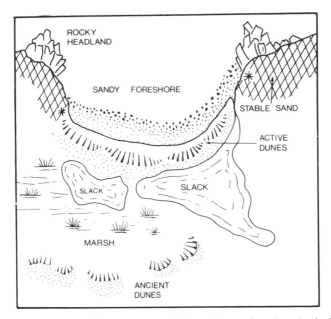

Fig.36. Map of a sand-dune system. The position of archaeological sites is shown by the asterisks; these were formerly inland on the edge of an ancient slack (cf. Fig.37).

for man. A system of this sort often occurs overlying Flandrian coastal sediments of both the eustatic and isostatic kind (Fig.35).

Evidence of an environmental/archaeological kind may be expected in one of three situations:

(1) Slack deposits exposed by stream erosion.
(2) The base of blow-outs in the active dune area.
(3) The periphery of the dune system where marine erosion is active.

The last situation, (3), has yielded some of the best sand-dune sites in Britain, notably Skara Brae in Orkney, and some of the most complete environmental successions, notably Northton in the Outer Hebrides (Evans, 1972a).

A vertical section through a deposit of coastal blown sand is likely to show a variety of environments (Fig.37). At the base there is generally a buried soil in which evidence of the pre-dune environment will be preserved. In some cases the initial sand accumulation

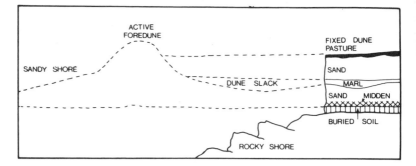

Fig.37. Section through a coastal blown sand deposit in an area in which sand is no longer accumulating. The present environment is a rocky shore with fixed-dune pasture (solid lines). The ancient environment from which these deposits derived was a sandy shore and active dune system (dashed lines). (From Spencer, 1975)

was slow enough to enable the incorporation of some sand into the buried soil by earthworm activity. If the sand is lime-rich, the calcium content of the buried soil will be upgraded, thus leading to the preservation of land molluscs (Evans, 1972a). These have provided interesting information about pre-dune environments in various parts of Britain — Cornwall, western Ireland, the Outer Hebrides and Orkney — suggesting that a vegetation cover of scrub or woodland may once have obtained in these now largely treeless areas (Spencer, 1975).

The main accumulation consists of layers of blown sand derived directly from the foreshore. The land mollusc faunas are of open-country type.

Intercalated buried soils reflecting standstill phases in sand deposition and stabilization of the land surface often occur. Land molluscs from these may indicate scrub/woodland regeneration in some instances.

Occasionally, freshwater marls reflecting periods of dune slack formation are exposed in section (Fig.37). The molluscan fauna of these is dominated by aquatic species.

At any level within the accumulation, archaeological horizons consisting of occupation debris, shell and bone middens, and houses may be expected. In some cases, as at Gwithian in Cornwall and Skaill in Orkney, prehistoric ploughmarks have been preserved in or beneath buried soils, attesting former cultivation.

Marine shellfish in archaeological levels deriving from man's food-gathering activities can provide additional data about shoreline changes — sandy or rocky — which can be tied in to the evidence derived from land molluscs and levels of sand deposition/soil formation (Evans, 1969) in the following way:

Coastline	Sand activity	Land molluscs	Shellfish
Sandy shore	Sand deposition	Open-country species	Sandy-shore species
Rocky shore	Soil formation	Woodland/scrub species	Rocky-shore species

Sand-dunes and deposits of coastal blown sand are an underrated and under-exploited source of environmental and archaeological data. The effect of sand deposition is to separate out occupation levels and environmental episodes which in a normal terrestrial situation become conflated into a single level.

River valleys (Gresswell, 1958a)

The remains of ancient river systems are preserved as *terraces* above the active flood plain or as *buried channels* beneath the modern river. Classically two types of river terrace are recognized, the *climatic* and the *thalassostatic*, the former independent of sea-level change, the latter controlled by it.

Climatic terraces form in the upper and middle reaches of a river away from tidal influence and the rejuvenating effects of downcutting. Typically, cold-climate deposits occur above those of warm-climate origin in any one terrace. The reasons for this are not fully understood, but the following model may be proposed. During a period of interglacial/temperate climate, deposits are laid down over a broad flood-plain by a slowly meandering river. Some downcutting takes place but there are many abandoned meanders (Fig.38). In an ensuing cold period there is a reduction in the amount of water entering the river, but at the same time the quantity of available rock debris is increased — as a result of intense frost-weathering and sparse vegetation cover. This material is borne by solifluxion and sudden spring thaws into the valley and deposited on top of the deposits of the previous temperate climate regime. There is no single river channel at this stage, the whole flood-plain consisting of a series of gravel banks and many small, ephemeral channels — a phenomenon known as braiding. Subsequently, a return to interglacial conditions leads to an increase in the volume of water coming into the river. Downcutting ensues and the deposits of the former interglacial/glacial cycle are left high and dry as terraces.

Thalassostatic terraces form in the lower reaches of a river where there is strong tidal influence, and where rejuvenation through glacial lowering of the sea takes place. Cold-climate deposits are generally found below warm-climate deposits in any one terrace. Again a simple model can be put forward. During an interglacial the river is sluggish and meandering (Fig.38), laying down fine sediments; the river is graded to sea-level in a shallow parabolic profile. During a glacial period of low sea-level, downcutting to a new base level takes place and a deep channel is formed (Fig.38). This gradually becomes choked with rock debris by solifluxion and meltwater activity in the same way as in the upper reaches. The flood-plain, once equilibrium is reached, presents the same braided appearance of gravel banks and a network of channels. Subsequent sea-level rise during an interglacial leads to the flooding of the cold-climate deposits, which thus come to occupy a *buried channel,* and their overlying by warm-climate muds. The flood-plain presents the same appearance as that described for the middle and upper reaches in an interglacial, with the additional complication of being tidal. This series of glacial/interglacial deposits is eventually left as a terrace during an ensuing glacial (Fig.38).

Pleistocene river systems, particularly during cold-climate periods, were dissimilar to those of today. The river course was less regular and often braided (Wymer, 1968). Banks of gravel, small pools, backswamp areas and active channels of swiftly flowing water occurred in no regular pattern. Thick deposits of gravel, so characteristic of Pleistocene river terraces all over the world, were laid down either during periods of cold climate or, if outside the periglacial zone, in periods of strongly seasonal climate in which intermittent high precipitation and violent flooding were characteristic features. Deep submerged channels of cold-climate origin, graded to low sea-level, are a feature of many river estuaries, for example the Severn and the Thames. In the case of the Severn, there is a channel 30 metres deep below the present river, the main reason for the steep incline and excessive length of the Severn railway tunnel.

Flood-plains were a typical environment of early man, particularly the Lower Palaeolithic hunters who, along with the animals they hunted, were no doubt attracted to them by the profusion of

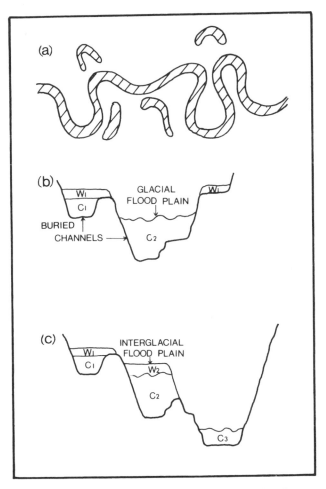

Fig.38. River terrace formation in the lower reaches of a river
(thalassostatic). (a) Plan of an interglacial flood-plain showing several
abandoned meanders. (b) Transverse section of river valley late on in a
glacial period when the buried channel has been cut and subsequently
choked with debris. (c) Transverse section early in the ensuing glacial
period after an intervening interglacial. w=warm- and c=cold-climate
deposits; the suffixes 1, 2 and 3 indicate successive glacial/interglacial
cycles.

habitats. The flint hand-axes of these groups, together with the
bones of large mammals, often abound in river gravels (Wymer,
1968). Later farming peoples also sought out the lower river

terraces because of their proximity to water, good drainage and high soil fertility. Alluvial deposits on the flood-plain were also settled but not so extensively, possibly because they are of relatively recent origin. It is interesting, however, that work in the Upper Thames Valley since 1962 has revealed a hitherto unsuspected wealth of cropmarks on the alluvium (Benson and Miles, 1974).

Very little work has been done on the origin, age and environment of recent flood loams. Pollen, macro-plant and snail analysis of deposits at Apethorpe in Northamptonshire suggest an origin extending back into the Boreal period (Sparks and Lambert, 1961). Other studies in the Worcestershire Avon by F. W. Shotton, and in Ireland (Mitchell, 1976) suggest a later date — Iron Age for the Avon, Early Bronze Age for a site in Co. Wexford, and early first millennium A.D. for the Boyne, all dates being radiocarbon assays of buried timber. It has been suggested, probably rightly, that these fine alluvial deposits are the result of a marked increase in the intensity of tillage on the valley sides, perhaps accompanied by an increase in rainfall. The resulting erosion and incorporation of debris into the rivers led to deposition further downstream. A marked change in the character of river valley floors probably took place between the early Flandrian and the period of increasing agricultural activity. Early on, flood-plains were probably of gravel with a braided and ill-defined course, rather like the situation in many highland regions today. Later, with the accumulation of much fine debris, the rivers probably became more canalized and the gravel buried. Embankment and the construction of flood dykes have probably contributed to their present-day state. Many early- and mid-Flandrian sites have probably been lost in this way. Another result of increasing downslope movement of soil into rivers has been the silting up of estuaries. Erstwhile coastal towns have become land-locked and river courses no longer navigable.

In the semi-arid Mediterranean zone these processes are more severe because of the greater intensity of erosion. This is due to the seasonal nature of the climate — long hot dry summers when the soil is dried and the vegetation parched, wet winters with sharp, heavy rain-storms. Two major phases of alluviation have been proposed (Vita-Finzi, 1969), one late Pleistocene, the other late Roman to medieval. It is likely that the later of these was brought about by deforestation and tillage. Recent work on Melos suggests an earlier, Bronze Age date for the onset of erosion there.

The processes of hillslope erosion and valley deposition have probably led, especially in Mediterranean countries, to a shift in prehistoric settlement patterns and economic strategies. Hillside farmsteads were abandoned in the face of increasing soil loss, and the valley bottoms more thickly populated. The change to richer, more moisture-retentive pastures may have necessitated a change of stock species — sheep/goat to cattle — and the different soils new types of crop.

Glaciers and ice-sheets (Gresswell, 1958b; West, 1968)

Glaciated landforms fall into two categories: those associated with *ice-sheets* and those associated with *valley glaciers*. In each case we can recognize *erosional* and *depositional* effects.

The general effect of an ice-sheet is to erode and make more uniform the land surface. Rocks over which ice has passed are often smoothed and are readily recognizable as ice-moulded. They were often selected by prehistoric man as ideal surfaces for his engravings, as is the case in Bronze Age Denmark.

The corries and U-valleys of highland regions are the most striking results of valley glaciation. The area at the foot of a corrie is generally overdeepened (Fig.39).

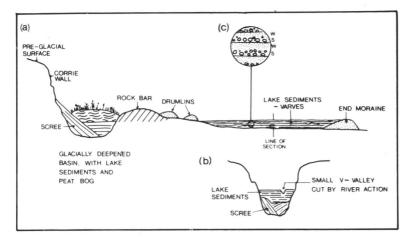

Fig.39. Various features associated with a glaciated valley. (a) Long section through a corrie and lower glaciated valley. (b) Section across sediments in the lower U-valley showing a later river-cut V-valley. (c) Enlarged section of varves in the ancient lake sediments; s=spring/summer; w=autumn/winter.

Depositional effects include the laying down of various types of boulder clay or till either as sheets (ground moraine) or as the more striking land forms of side and end moraines — great banks of debris at the edges or toe of a glacier. The end moraines associated with the wastage of the Last Glaciation ice-sheets constitute very prominent features of the landscape in North America and northern Europe.

Erosional features associated with differential thicknesses of ice often become water-filled after the ice has melted. These are *corrie lakes* — dammed by a rock or moraine bar; *kettle holes* — where greater thicknesses of ice (generally of an ice-sheet) took longer to melt; and *fjords* or *sea lochs* — in effect U-valleys which have subsequently been flooded by sea-level rise (Fig.39).

Other depositional features of glacial origin are *drumlins* and *eskers*. Drumlins are egg-shaped mounds of either sand and gravel or morainic material formed characteristically at the head of a U-valley (Fig.39) or in an area of ice-sheet wastage. Extensive drumlin fields are characteristic of northern and western Ireland. Eskers are long sinuous banks of sand and gravel which formed sub-glacially (i.e. beneath a glacier) along the course of a river — in other words the casts of sub-glacial rivers. They may be several metres high and often a kilometre or more in length, forming prominent landscape features. The related features known as *kames* form in a similar manner but along the edge of a glacier.

Another feature of glacial origin is the so-called *glacial overflow channel*. The damming of river courses by an ice-sheet leads in some cases to the formation of extensive systems of *glacial lakes*, each overflowing to a lower level and creating deep overflow channels in the process. Such systems have been described from north-east Yorkshire, the north Dyfed coast, and around the Wicklow Mountains in eastern Ireland. Recent work, however, has shown that at least some of these — particularly the Dyfed group — are either sub-glacial or latero-glacial features having formed beneath or lateral to a glacier (John, 1970).

Immediately beyond the limits of a glacier or ice-sheet, extensive spreads of *glacial outwash sands and gravels* were laid down. Sometimes this material was deposited in a lake (Fig.39) in a strongly layered form as *varves* — the word varve is Scandinavian for a layer. Coarse sediments of sand and coarse silt were deposited during the periods of spring melt, finer silts and clays during the summer. No sediment at all was laid down during the winter freeze. Each varve or layer is thus double and represents one year; its total thickness is climatically controlled, depending on the degree and vigour of the spring melt. Varve deposits therefore have important climatic implications. They also provide a dating mechanism along lines similar to dendrochonology, and before the advent of radiocarbon were the main yardstick for the later stages of the Ice Age in northern Europe.

The effects of glaciation are of importance to the subsequent human occupants of an area. The deposition of morainic material results in the redistribution of the geological bedrock which in some cases is beneficial, in others detrimental, to the subsequent soil type. For example, calcareous boulder clay transported into a region of acidic rocks will make soils more suitable for farming communities, although less so for hunter–gatherers (p.6).

Sea lochs, U-valleys, and sub- and latero-glacial channels are significant in terms of communications and localizing settlement. Glacial lakes and kettle holes add an important element of variability to the environment, whose significance is discussed later, in the section on lakes (p.105).

Periglacial features (West, 1968; Williams, 1973)

On the whole, the events that took place outside the area of glaciation but where the climate was less than temperate — the *periglacial zone* — have made comparatively little impact on the landscape. Three main groups of features can be recognized:

(1) Depositional.
    (a) Loess and coversand.
    (b) Solifluxion deposits.
(2) Erosional — mainly associated with solifluxion.
(3) Frost, or cryoturbation, structures.
    (a) Ice wedges.
    (b) Pingos.
    (c) Involutions.

The formation of *loess* and *coversand* has already been discussed. Both occur as thick sheets of sediment, the former mainly in central and eastern Europe, with isolated patches as far west as south-east England — notably Pegwell Bay — and the latter to the north and west. Like the deposits of coastal sand already discussed, loess is of vital importance in environmental archaeology in providing long sequences of prehistoric environments particularly for the Upper Palaeolithic. Among the best-known sites is that of Dolni Vestonice in Moravia where an Upper Palaeolithic mammoth-kill floor was revealed more or less as abandoned tens of thousands of years ago (Klima, *et al.*, 1962). Land surfaces are buried with little or no disturbance. In Germany, Austria and Czechoslovakia the sequence of buried soils — brownearths and chernozems — preserved within the loess has been used to reconstruct the characteristics of the warm-climate episodes — e.g. whether of interglacial or interstadial status, and what sort of vegetation they supported — steppe or woodland, etc. Land molluscs are often well preserved in loess and have been widely used in Czechoslovakia as environmental and climatic indicators (Lozêk, 1967). On the whole, loess and cover-sand are associated with cold, dry climates.

By contrast, the processes of *solifluxion* require a cold, moist climate. Solifluxion debris — the mechanism of solifluxion has already been described — occurs on a much more localized scale than loess. It is far more typical of western Europe and mountain areas. Due to the disturbance of the ground, buried land surfaces are only preserved in the finer deposits — sometimes called *melt-water muds and gravels* (Kerney, 1963). These occur, as we shall see, at the base of dry valley successions (p.99). Indeed, the main erosional effects of the periglacial landscape are associated with solifluxion and the formation of dry valleys — particularly in chalk and limestone country where later stream modification has been slight.

Cryoturbation structures (Williams, 1973) form under various different climatic and environmental conditions. *Ice wedges* (Fig.41) are indicative of permafrost and require a mean annual temperature of −6 to −9°C. The low temperatures of the arctic winters cause the ground to shrink and crack, often to depths of several metres. During spring, melting of the surface layers of the ground fills the crack with water which subsequently freezes, further enlarging the crack. In this way a wedge of ice forms, and the pattern that several ice wedges make is a characteristic network, often polygonal (Fig.40). In Britain, of course, there are no ice wedges today but the casts of former Pleistocene examples do occur, particularly on river gravels. Their possible confusion with, and distinction from, man-made features is discussed later (p.119).

Pingos are lenses of ice which form below the ground, particularly in very wet areas. As the lens grows, the ground is pushed up and soil and rock slips off to form an enclosing ring. On melting, a pond forms where the ice lens was formerly, surrounded by a ring of soil and rock. Again there is some possibility of confusion with man-made features, particularly with ring cairns and henges, and they can give trouble when seen for the first time if not recognized for what they are.

The last category of periglacial structures to be discussed is the *involution*. Some of these are seen in section in Fig.41. They form under milder climatic conditions than ice wedges, and generally

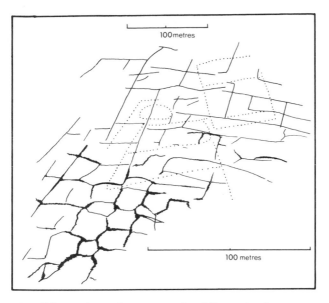

Fig.40. Fossil ice-wedge polygons seen in oblique air view as cropmarks. Moulton, Northamptonshire. Dotted lines indicate later archaeological features. (From Evans, 1972b, after a photograph by R. Hollowell)

only in the *active layer* where thawing takes place in spring. It is not known precisely how involutions form, but differential freezing and thawing of two different sediment types probably builds up stresses which cause the underlying sediment to push upwards and occlude the overlying deposit as characteristic flask-shaped forms. Involutions form polygonally-patterned ground — on a much smaller scale than ice wedges — which on slopes becomes elongated to form *stripes*. In very stony upland areas involutions may appear in plan as *stone rings* (cf. Fig.41).

Dry valleys

Dry valleys are particularly characteristic of chalk and limestone areas and are most strikingly developed along the steep scarp-slope zones. They may carry streams, but on the whole these are incidental to the original formation of the valley which was through the process of solifluxion along planes of weakness in the rock (Kerney, *et al.*, 1964).

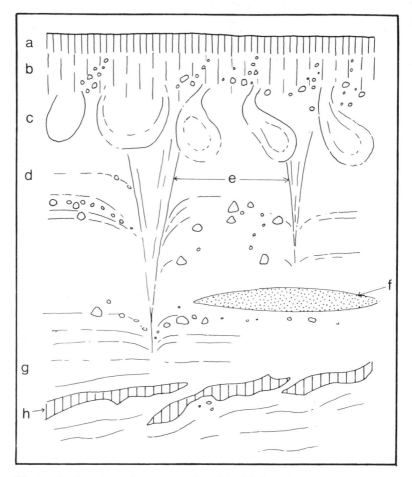

Fig.41. Section through a series of periglacial deposits and features.
(a) Modern soil. (b) 'Flames' of unweathered stones in the base of the modern soil; in upland regions with thin soil cover these would appear in plan as stone rings. (c) Involutions. (d) Coarse solifluxion gravel.
(e) Ice-wedge casts. (f) Silt (loess) lens. (g) Fine solifluxion (meltwater) gravel. (h) Buried soil, contorted and faulted by frost action and solifluxion.

The sequences of sediments preserved in the dry valleys of southern Britain comprises three main series (Fig.42):

(1) A basal series of periglacial deposits.

(2)   A series of calcareous tufas in the central section.
(3)   An upper series of hillwashes.

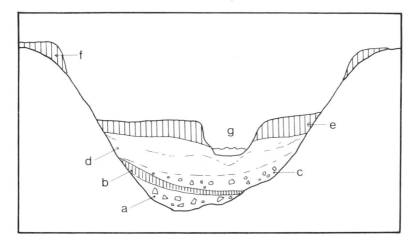

Fig.42. Cross section of Late-Devensian and Flandrian deposits in a
limestone dry valley in southern Britain. (a) Periglacial scree, Late-
Devensian zone I. (b) Buried soil, zone II (Allerød). (c) Periglacial
scree, zone III. (d) Tufa, Pre-boreal to Atlantic; generally with
intercalated buried soils. (e) Hillwash, Neolithic onwards.
(f) Accumulation of hillwash at the break of slope between plateau and
dry valley sides; Neolithic onwards. (g) Present-day river valley; not
always present, particularly in chalk country.

Typically the basal series consists of screes or fine solifluxion debris
with one or more intercalated buried soils. On molluscan, stratigraphical and radiocarbon evidence, these deposits can usually be
ascribed to the Late-Devensian, with the main buried soil being of
Allerød (zone II) age. In exceptional cases there may be earlier, full
glacial, deposits of coombe rock (coarse chalky solifluxion debris),
loess and/or coversand.

The overlying tufas, which sometimes attain thicknesses of over
five metres, are of early- to mid-Flandrian age, again being dated
on molluscan and radiocarbon evidence. As already described, tufa
forms under warm, humid climatic conditions in an environment of
shaded marsh or swamp. The deposit is essentially a terrestrial one.
An early phase of open woodland has been detected in some sites.
Freshwater horizons and buried soils reflect respectively, flooding
and drying out of the environment, and the latter may be

climatically controlled. There is sometimes a prominent soil horizon part way through the tufa sequence which may be equated with the known period of late Boreal dryness.

Mesolithic flint artefacts and the bones of large mammals such as wild ox have sometimes been recovered from deposits of tufa and their associated soils. Indeed, in some cases the abandonment of an area by man may have been a direct result of the onset of tufa formation.

The division between the tufa and hillwash is usually marked by a pronounced buried soil, generally dating to the later part of the Flandrian — Neolithic or Bronze Age times. This represents a period of stability between the cessation of tufa formation and the commencement of hillwashing. Why tufa no longer forms in the British Isles is not entirely clear but a climatic cause — insufficiently high temperatures — is probably in part responsible. The hillwash is largely anthropogenic in origin, being brought about by tillage or animal overgrazing is already explained (p.70). On the whole, the land molluscs from the buried soil indicate woodland giving way to open ground (Fig.22) — another result of man's activities — and the hillwash contains artefacts ranging from the Neolithic to Iron Age (and exceptionally later) periods.

Study of these deposits is best done by molluscan analysis, and the main zones, both environmental and molluscan, are shown in Table 2. In limestone — as opposed to chalk — areas, where caves open out onto the side of a dry valley (Fig.43), it would be interesting to investigate both valley and cave deposits in order to correlate the two successions (see p.102), and amplify the cave sequence with the undoubtedly longer record from the dry valley. Unfortunately, and rather surprisingly, this has never been attempted in Britain.

Caves, rock-shelters and fissures (Schmid, 1969)

There is a whole variety of what can be described as 'natural underground shelters' from the shallow rock-shelter (or *abri*) to the total cave, and their modes of formation are various. It is useful to distinguish the *sea cave* and the *inland cave*, although the latter is often coastal. The classification refers to their mode of formation.

Sea caves are carved out, generally along planes of weakness in the rock, by marine action, and may be formed in any rock of sufficient hardness to support a cave. Their length is finite, and, unless connected by a blowhole to the terrestrial ambience, they have only one entrance. Most are associated with raised shore-lines — either Flandrian or Last Interglacial — as already discussed (Fig.34).

Inland caves are typically abandoned underground river systems

Table 2. Succession of environmental episodes in a dry valley in southern Britain.

Deposit	Environment	Molluscan fauna	Zonation
Hillwash	Open-country/ arable	*Vallonia, Pupilla, Helicella*	Sub-atlantic/ Sub-boreal
Buried soil	Forest clearance	*Pomatias elegans*	Sub-boreal
Tufa	Woodland	*Discus rotundatus, Pomatias elegans, Acanthinula lamellata*	Atlantic
		Discus ruderatus, Vertigo genesii	Boreal
	Open woodland		Pre-boreal
Scree/ Meltwater deposits	Grassland/ Tundra/ Birch copses	*Helicella itala, Abida secale*	Late-glacial
Coversands/ Coombe rock	Arctic desert	No fauna	Full glacial

which have been cut into by subsequent erosion — coastal, riverine or solifluxion — and exposed. A characteristic situation, and one favoured by early man, is where a cave mouth opens onto the side of a valley, at the base of a cliff and the top of a scree slope (Fig.43). The entrance is often small or constricted but may open out considerably in the interior. The length of the cave may be indefinite, and the ramifications of the system complex. It was caves of this sort that were utilized by the Franco-Cantabrian Upper Palaeolithic artists to depict their masterpiece paintings and engravings. These were sometimes made hundreds of metres from the cave entrance.

In some instances the mouth of the cave is enlarged through proximity to atmospheric processes of weathering and erosion — mainly frost-shattering and gravity (Fig.43). In these cases a *rock shelter* forms and this is often most suitable for human occupation. Many of the French Upper Palaeolithic *abris* are of this type. Occupation debris and deposits suitable for environmental study may accumulate on the floor of the rock shelter and outside the

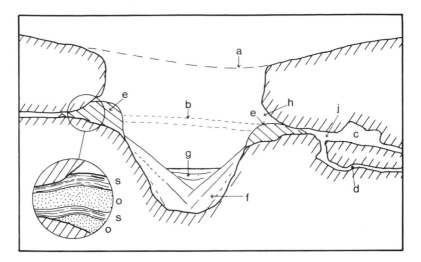

Fig.43. Section through an inland cave system and dry valley. (a) Land surface during cave formation. (b) Old underground river course. (c) Chamber. (d) Later river course. (e) Talus cone outside cave. (f) Dry valley deposits, mainly scree. (g) Recent valley sediments (cf. Fig.42). (h) Rock shelter. (j) Passage. (o) Occupation debris. (s) Stalagmite.

mouth as a debris cone spilling down into the valley. The floor of the shelter is gradually raised and, in exceptional cases, the entrance totally blocked. As already suggested, study of the dry valley sediments would undoubtedly provide complementary information and expand the sequence.

The main and most characteristic types of cave sediment are stalagmite, breccia and cave earth, although others more familiar from open-air situations may occur, including fluviatile and pond deposits, wind-blown sands and silts, and buried soils. It is sometimes useful to consider the deposits in terms of those that are derived *in situ* from the cave roof and walls or by chemical weathering — *autochthonous* deposits; and those that are brought in from outside — *allochthonous* deposits.

Two further points special to the study of cave deposits need mention. One concerns the formation of stalagmite. As already discussed this material forms under humid and fairly equable climatic conditions. It does not form when intense frost-shattering is taking place. Sequences of alternate stalagmite and breccia layers are typical of many caves. But stalagmite is not always a good indicator of contemporary climate since the accumulation of deposits around a cave mouth may ultimately block the entrance, sealing off the cave interior and creating far more equable climatic conditions inside than outside the cave. It is quite feasible in these circumstances that stalagmite formation inside and scree formation outside could be taking place at precisely the same time.

The other point concerns the non-human occupants. Large carnivores, especially bears and hyenas, are characteristic cave inhabitants, and much of the bone debris in the deposits may therefore derive from animal rather than human meals. It is only through careful quantitative studies of associated artefacts, charcoal and so forth, that the different origins of the bone remains can be assessed (Fig.14).

Fissures are of various origins. Often they result from various forms of physical fracturing of the rock, for example along planes of weakness — generally more or less vertical — caused by folding or faulting. Sometimes they are of more complex origin and form part of an interlocking system of abandoned underground rivers. The process of formation and infill of fissures has been particularly well studied in the case of the early man/Australopithecine sites in southern Africa (Sampson, 1974), and the main stages are as follows (Fig.44):

(1) Formation and abandonment of underground river. Deposition of residual riverine/pond sediments.
(2) Link with the surface through cracks which enlarge at first by groundwater percolation leading to stalagmite formation, and later by subaerial weathering to form fissures or *avens*. The material from these processes accumulates as a cone of stalagmite, breccia and cave earth.
(3) Exposure of the fissure and cave deposits by valley erosion.

During stage (2), human occupation debris may become incorporated into the deposits from the surface, but on the whole the system was not inhabited. This is an important difference between fissures and rock shelters.

It is relevant to mention that probably the earliest artefacts to have been found in Britain — several flint flakes of crude workmanship — have been recovered from a fissure at Westbury-sub-Mendip in Somerset (Bishop, 1974). They are probably of Cromerian age.

Lakes

Lakes form in a variety of situations. Some, like Lake Eyre in

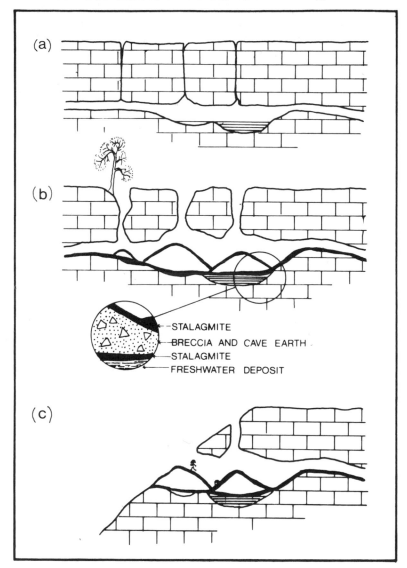

Fig.44. Stages in the formation of a cave and fissure system.
(a) Formation of underground river (cave) and deposition of freshwater deposits. Cracks in limestone not yet opened. (b) Opening of cracks to form fissures (avens) linking cave with surface. Abandonment of river and formation of stalagmite layers and debris cones beneath avens.
(c) Valley erosion exposing fissure and cave system. Occupation by man may take place at this stage.

Australia, Lake Chad and Lake Baikal, are of ancient geological origin, being controlled by depressions in the parent rock. Others are found in rift valleys (p.110) and are of more recent origin, notably the great series in East Africa. Blocked overflows may be caused by morainic material or glacial over-deepening; Derwent Water and others in the English Lake District are of this origin. Some may be due to the deposition of volcanic material — ash or lava; the sediments at Olduvai Gorge in the East African rift valley system are in part of lacustrine origin, formed initially by the blocking of a river by a lava flow. The Mesolithic settlement of Thatcham in Berkshire was beside a lake possibly caused by a beaver dam.

Lakes are important for a variety of reasons. They provide a supply of water, and good and reliable communications. They add variety to the habitat, not only in their more obvious aquatic attributes like fish, water fowl and so on, but also in the edge communities of reedswamp, marsh, fen and carr.

To the archaeologist they are important in that they provide a catchment for environmental indicators of a whole variety of types, and, along the shore, of archaeological material also. The prima site of Star Carr was of this type — bone, antler, wood, pollen and macroscopic plant remains such as birch bark and seeds, as well as the usual stone artefacts, were well preserved here (Clark, 1954). Methods of study of lake sediments include pollen analysis, diatom, cladoceran and molluscan investigations, as well as various chemical techniques for measuring halides — chlorine and iodine — other mineral elements and organic matter. Halides are possible climatic indicators, particularly if a lake is close to the sea, being deposited from rain during periods of oceanicity. Many other factors, however, may be responsible for variations in the halide content of lake sediments (Mackereth, 1966). High organic content is a possible index of soil erosion — and human agricultural activity — on the hill-slopes around a lake.

In theory, and often in practice, lakes are ephemeral, and over the ages become infilled with sediments and eventually dry up altogether. The pollen diagram in Fig.3 is from ancient lake sediments in Nant Ffrancon, North Wales. A typical sequence of events in a glacially formed lake might be as follows (Fig.45):

(1) Glacial till is overlain by outwash sands and gravels laid down by the wasting glacier.
(2) There follows a series of lake sediments which are of late-glacial origin. Organic horizons reflect periods of climatic warmth and the absence of physical weathering; solifluxion

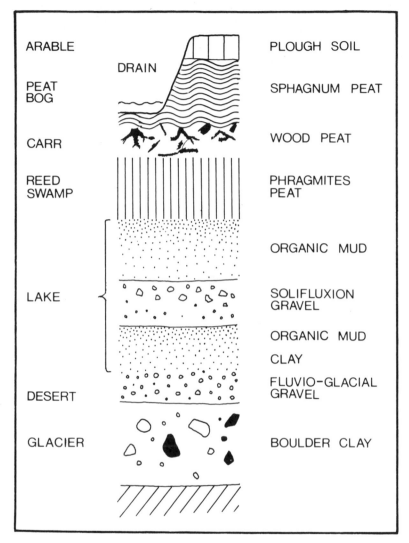

Fig.45. Generalized section through ancient lake sediments in a formerly glaciated basin (cf. Fig.39). The clay/organic mud/solifluxion gravel succession is typical of such sequences in Britain and reflects the Late-Devensian zones I, II and III (cf. Fig.42).

gravels, periods of mass wasting.
(3) Flandrian lake muds gradually become more organic as the lake shallows, and eventually give way to reedswamp peat.
(4) True terrestrial conditions are eventually attained with alder carr forming wood peat.
(5) Raising of the bog surface by continued peat formation leads to acidity, destruction of the carr, and the development of impoverished *Sphagnum* bog.
(6) Drainage and the addition of fertilizers enables the land to be cultivated.

In the later stages of this succession, the various plant communities were, and still are, exploited by man — reeds for thatch and bedding, brushwood for kindling, fencing and small artefacts, peat for fuel.

In Ireland and south-west Scotland wooden island dwellings known as *crannogs* were often sited in shallow lakes during later prehistoric and early historic times. They have been little studied due to difficulties of excavation, many still being in active lakes, but those that have been excavated have yielded a wealth of organic artefactual and environmental data. One of the earliest records of insect remains from an archaeological site was from Lochlee Crannog in Ayrshire.

Peat bogs (Godwin, 1956)

The characteristics of peat as a sediment have already been described. Peat forms in two types of situation, *ombrogenous* and *topogenous*.

Ombrogenous peat forms under conditions of high rainfall irrespective of topography. It spreads over plateau and valley alike and is often known as *blanket peat*. A typical section of blanket peat (Fig.46) shows a free-draining soil profile on rock, overlain by wood peat and tree stools of birch and occasional pine. Above this is the ombrogenous peat made up largely of *Sphagnum* moss, *Eriophorum* (cotton grass — actually a sedge), and heather. All these plants are tolerant of acid soil conditions and are pretty undemanding in their nutrient requirements. This is a reflection of the fact that ombrogenous peat communities derive practically all their nutrients and moisture from the atmosphere.

Two layers may generally be discerned in ombrogenous peat sections, a lower *Sphagnum* peat (LSP) in which plant remains are well decomposed and often unrecognizable as such, and an upper *Sphagnum* peat (USP) where there is much less decomposition and

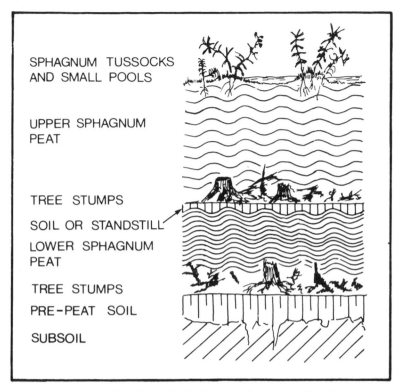

SPHAGNUM TUSSOCKS
AND SMALL POOLS

UPPER SPHAGNUM
PEAT

TREE STUMPS

SOIL OR STANDSTILL

LOWER SPHAGNUM
PEAT

TREE STUMPS

PRE-PEAT SOIL

SUBSOIL

Fig.46. Typical section through blanket peat in western Britain.

where recognizable stems and leaves are present. The boundary between the two layers is marked by a very dark, almost amorphous, upper surface to the LSP which reflects a period of drying out of the bog surface, and in which the stumps of pine are sometimes preserved, reflecting a local colonization of the bog surface by trees. Above is the very fibrous USP representing renewed peat growth and known as a *recurrence surface*. Many such boundaries are known from the bogs of north-west Europe and they are not all of the same age; sometimes there may be more than one in the same bog sequence. The recurrence surfaces number at least five (they are sometimes known as RYs after the Scandinavian *recurrenzytor*), and the third, dated to around the middle of the first millennium B.C. is known as the *grenzhorizont*. This is usually taken as the transition between the Sub-boreal and Sub-atlantic periods, although recent work suggests a somewhat earlier and less precise date for this transition.

Topogenous peat forms in basin situations and is controlled by topography. Typical situations are kettle holes, infilled lakes and coastal flats, and the peat communities are dominated by a greater variety of plants than found in ombrogenous peat, and by plants more demanding in their nutrient — particularly calcium — requirements. The Somerset Levels is a typical region of topogenous peat formation and the general sequence is similar to that shown in the upper levels of Fig.45 in which the sediments of an infilled lake basin are depicted. Acid *Sphagnum* peat horizons form when the level of the peat surface rises above the influence of ground water, but frequent floodings by calcareous water lead to a recurrence of topogenous peat formation in which species such as the sedge, *Cladium mariscus*, are prolific.

Prehistoric *wooden trackways* are occasionally found in peat bogs, usually in the course of peat cutting. The best-known series comes from the Somerset Levels where trackways of various ages ranging from the early Neolithic to the Iron Age survive. A variety of constructional methods was used, some of them extremely elaborate, particularly the raised walkway of the Sweet Track (Coles, *et al.*, 1973). Some of the earlier trackways are within the carr or fen wood stage, and may have been built as the reedswamp dwindled in area and transport by boat became increasingly difficult. In other words, they were built in response to a *drying* environment. By contrast, some of the later examples appear to have been built in association with flooding horizons and thus during a time when the environment was becoming *wetter*. However, economic factors, such as the need to take in some of the raised islands of drier ground in the peat bog for tillage, or an increase in fowling activities, may have dictated the need for a trackway, irrespective of climatic or environmental change.

Volcanic situations

Volcanic sediments comprise lava, ash and other pyroclastic deposits — that is, deposits shot out rather than poured out — in which large stones, or volcanic bombs, abound. There is a whole variety of fields in which volcanic activity impinges on man. The following are some of the more important:

(1) Dating (West, 1968).
    (a) Potassium–argon.
    (b) Tephrochronology.
(2) Sealing archaeological layers.
(3) Upgrading soils.
(4) Production of economically valuable rocks.

Potassium–argon dating is based on the alteration of the isotope potassium-40 to argon. The main assumptions on which the method depends are (a) that the decay process takes place at a known rate, and (b) that fresh volcanic deposits contain no argon. The method has been used to date several early man and Australopithecine sites in East Africa and south-east Asia, and it has shown that the evolution of early forms of man extended into the Tertiary period, perhaps as early as five million years ago.

Tephrochronology is more of a relative dating technique in which widespread ash falls can be identified mineralogically and thus be used as marker horizons. One such in the Eifel region of north Germany has been dated to zone II of the late-glacial, the Allerød period.

Well-known examples of the burial and superb preservation of archaeological horizons by volcanic ash deposits are the Roman towns of Herculaneum and Pompeii. The Olduvai Gorge sequence includes several layers of volcanic sediment, no doubt one of the reasons for the richness of the area in fossil material.

The attractions to man of volcanic regions are twofold. In the first place, for farming communities, the soils are exceptionally rich in minerals, and provide excellent conditions for plant and crop growth. Secondly, the use of various volcanic rocks by early man — obsidian for knives and mirrors, lava for querns — has always been important (p.6). At the early Neolithic town of Çatal Hüyük in Anatolia there is a wall painting depicting a volcanic eruption, possibly a votive or magical representation to an important source of material equipment (Mellaart, 1967).

Volcanic environments may also have been significant in the early stages of human evolution, particularly in rift valley situations. Volcanic eruptions cause violent and marked habitat change — rivers alter course, lakes form, land is engulfed by lava and inundated by ash. Forest fires break out and early forms of man may have needed to flee the wooded valleys and spread onto the savanna plains. Habitat changes such as these would have required new adaptations, and may have brought about or at least speeded up human evolution, as well as the evolution of associated game animals.

Rift valleys

Rift valleys are ideal catchment areas for environmental and archaeological material, and their importance has become paramount since the East African discoveries of early man sites at Olduvai, East Rudolph and Omo. Rift valleys form along major faults or vertical planes of weakness in the earth's crust. They are elongated zones of environmental instability where volcanic activity, the rapid formation and equally rapid disappearance of lakes, and faulting take place. They are areas where environmental change is persistent and dramatic. Such situations lead not only to the rapid buildup of sediments and the incorporation of archaeological and environmental evidence, but also to faulting and downcutting which result in the exposure and discovery of this material as in the 100-metre section at Olduvai Gorge.

Often associated with rift valleys and volcanic activity are *playa lakes*. These are ephemeral, sometimes being formed in the first instance by the blocking of a river by a lava flow, and are characteristic of semi-arid climates where the rainfall is very intermittent. They are often saline and have characteristic fauna and flora. During periods of dryness, *salt crusts* form over the surface layers by evaporation.

In East Africa the main early man sites occur in the eastern or Gregory rift. The deposits infilling the rift are various types of lake, fluviatile, deltaic and marsh sediment, and successions hundreds of metres thick have been recorded. These are often fragmented, occurring as blocks, or *inselbergs,* isolated by down-faulting of adjacent sediment. Correlation from one exposure to another is made on the basis of the fauna and marker horizons of volcanic tuff or ash. Some sequences go back over five million years.

The first site to be investigated was Olduvai Gorge. Here, L.S.B. Leakey and his wife unearthed an early hominid skull known as *Australopithecus* (formerly *Zinjanthropus*) *boisei*, dating to approximately 1·8 million years. An associated form, *Homo habilis*, had a higher brain capacity and was thought to have made the stone tools found with the skeletal remains. Next to be investigated were deposits in the Omo River valley in southern Ethiopia, where a French team has found evidence of a variety of Australopithecine forms. The most recent work, by R.E.F. Leakey, has been on the eastern shores of Lake Rudolph (Lake Turkana) and here an early hominid, more advanced and with a higher cranial capacity than the Australopithecines, has been discovered, dating to about 2·8 million years.

These exciting discoveries have only been made possible by the long and relatively complete series of deposits laid down in the rift valley during the Pleistocene and preceeding Tertiary periods.

6 Archaeological situations

Various archaeological features yield environmental information, some of which may be of regional significance and some of relevance only to the special environment created by the feature itself. This applies particularly to hollows such as ditches and shafts where local environmental conditions of extreme moisture override the general ambience, as we shall see. But it is less well appreciated that the problem may also arise in the study of buried soils. Although it is attractive to consider the segment of land surface sealed by a round barrow as a reflection of at least one part of the Bronze Age environment, it is not necessarily the case, and in fact was almost certainly not the case, that barrows were sited at random either with regard to topography, vegetation or land-use history. It is therefore necessary to look at other Bronze Age features — pits, linear earthworks and lynchets — to get a realistic overview of the various environmental facets of the time.

Bank and ditch situations

Field monuments of the bank and ditch type include barrows, linear earthworks, and various enclosures such as causewayed camps, hill-forts and motte-and-bailey castles. Environmental information can be derived from two main sources:

(1) The buried soil beneath the bank or mound.
(2) The ditch sediments.

These two sources are complementary in providing a sequence of environmental history bracketing the site. The buried soil yields information about the pre-site environment and land use; the ditch sediments about the post-site history.

A third, lesser, source of information is the earthwork bank or mound itself.

Buried soils beneath earthworks (Dimbleby and Speight, 1969)

The main types of soil and some of their physical and chemical

112

properties have been discussed in Chapter 4. In the last chapter, several examples of the association of buried soils with various sediment types were cited. Here we are concerned specifically with soils beneath archaeological monuments.

On the whole, in north-west Europe, there are three types of chemical environment in which buried soils on archaeological sites occur — basic, neutral and acid. *Basic soils* are characteristic of limestone, chalk and calcareous sediments like loess and tufa. The main biological material used in their interpretation is the molluscs. *Acid soils*, of the podsol group, are characteristic of impoverished sands and sandstones, or areas of high rainfall. The main biological indicators are pollen and charcoal. *Neutral soils* occur on relatively rich subsoils, but without the high calcium carbonate content that gives rise to the rendsina. There are no characteristic biological indicators. In exceptional cases, where the soil beneath an archaeological monument is anaerobic — e.g. Silbury Hill — insect and macroscopic plant remains will be preserved as well. Therefore, as far as buried soils are concerned, we can recognize four types of depositional environment, each of which has its own characteristic biological indicators.

Aerobic/basic	*Aerobic/acid*	*Aerobic/neutral*	*Anaerobic*
Molluscs	Pollen	Charcoal	Pollen
Bones	Charcoal	(Pollen)	Charcoal
Charcoal		(Bone)	Molluscs
(Pollen)			Bone
			Macro-plants
			Insects

Indicators in brackets are of minimal value but may be used on occasion. The groupings, of course, apply to other environmental situations of similar chemical attributes, but it is useful to consider and summarize them here.

An important feature of buried soils preserved beneath arch-aeological sites is that they are generally at a higher level than the ambient modern soil (Fig.47). This phenomenon is known as *differential weathering* and is due to the protection of the subsoil by the archaeological monument (Atkinson, 1957; Darwin, 1881). Lowering of the surrounding, unprotected, area is due to the various processes of weathering and erosion. Differences of up to one metre between ancient and modern surfaces are recorded. On calcareous subsoils, solution is largely responsible for this difference, although cultivation around a monument may be a contributory factor. On siliceous gravels and other acidic subsoils, tillage and deflation of the surface by wind erosion are probably the main agents. Thus not only is the buried soil preserved with all its concomitant biological and morphological indicators; a section of the subsoil, albeit of slight thickness, is present also (Fig.47), elsewhere having been destroyed. This is of value in yielding information about the late Pleistocene and early Flandrian history of an area, and about the immediate parent material of the buried soil.

The importance of buried soils, not only to environmental archaeology but to the whole study of our ecological history, is only just beginning to be realized widely. And it is those preserved beneath archaeological sites that have provided some of the best results. Archaeologists and natural scientists alike must be aware of their far-reaching value. Bogs and lake sediments may have provided splendid zonal sequences of vegetation throughout the world, but in the last few years buried soils have yielded the answers to some of the most pressing problems of our landscape history. Fine sampling and detailed analysis of pollen and land snails from soils *in immediate association with archaeological sites* have shed whole new light on the recent ecological history of the loess (Lozêk, 1964), the chalklands (Evans, 1972a) and the acid soils of heath and moor (Dimbleby, 1962).

Ditches (Cornwall, 1958; Limbrey, 1975)

With the exception of buried soils, ditches are the most useful archaeological feature in yielding regional information. This is particularly the case with the larger ditches of long barrows, hillforts and mottes in which sedimentation may be prolonged and the effects of local conditions minimized by the shallow profile, especially in the upper stages of infilling. Three main stages can be recognized (Fig.47):

(1) The primary and secondary fill.
(2) The buried soil.
(3) The tertiary fill.

In the first winter after a ditch is dug, frost-weathering attacks the sides and causes large fragments of rock to fall and accumulate in the ditch angles. Undercutting of the topsoil causes turves to become incorporated in subsequent years — valuable evidence of the pre-site environment if the bank and buried soil beneath it have

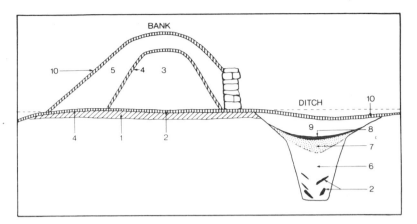

Fig.47. Transverse section through a bank and ditch. (1) Thin layer of Pleistocene deposits preserved only beneath bank. (2) Pre-bank buried soil and fallen turves in ditch. (3) First phase bank. (4) Turf on first phase bank. (5) Second phase bank. (6) Primary fill of second phase ditch. (7) Secondary fill. (8) Buried soil in ditch. (9) Ploughwash, tertiary fill. (10) Modern topsoil.

been destroyed. This coarse frost-shattered fill and associated turves is the *primary fill*. Observations on open cuttings and the ditches of *experimental earthworks* built specifically to study these weathering processes suggest a period of between ten and twenty years for its formation (Evans and Limbrey, 1975; Jewell and Dimbleby, 1966).

Similar weathering processes, aided by rainwashing and earthworm upcasting, lead to the formation of the *secondary fill*. This takes place on a gentler scale because much of the original ditch sides is now protected and the gradient less steep. The secondary fill is finer material, more humic than the primary fill, and more likely to yield biological environmental indicators. On the whole, however, these will be of limited regional value because of the special nature of the ditch environment at this stage — initially an unstable surface with sparse vegetational cover, later becoming more overgrown but strongly influenced by shelter and a greater humidity than the general ambience. The similarity of numerous molluscan diagrams from ditches of a whole variety of ages — Neolithic to Medieval — underlines this point clearly (Evans, 1972a).

As the gradient of the ditch sides becomes less steep, however, evidence of a more regional type may be expected. Ultimately deposition ceases and a *soil* forms (Fig.47). This is the stage reached by many upland sites today in which there is still a well-defined ditch, and in which the modern soil directly overlies the secondary fill.

The third and final stage — if it occurs at all — is generally of man-made origin, and generally caused by agriculture. Thick deposits of ploughwash, sometimes with intercalated soils reflecting periods of non-tillage, are recorded from numerous sites. The ditch is practically obliterated. This material is the *tertiary fill*. It often contains datable artefacts, notably pottery sherds spread onto the fields with domestic rubbish used as manure.

Study of ditch sediments is best done through an investigation of the morphological properties of the soils and sediments in the field and of their chemical and physical properties in the laboratory. On chalk and limestone, snail analysis can be applied. But on acid sites, even pollen analysis is rarely of value, due to the diverse origin of the pollen (cf. p.24).

Anaerobic ditch sediments

In lowlying situations, particularly on river gravel, or where a ditch is exceptionally deep, some of the deposits may be waterlogged. A variety of organic indicators may be expected, and the possibilities of checking and complementing the evidence of one with the other are manifold. A typical sequence is as follows (cf. Fig.49):

(1) Aerobic *primary fill*, generally coarse gravel.
(2) *Anaerobic fill* of plant debris, other organic matter, and occupation rubbish which may enhance the anaerobic state. Environmental evidence is obtained from macroscopic plant remains and insects (cf. Fig.49).
(3) *Semi-waterlogged clays*, probably in part water-lain, and appearing as orange/grey mottled in section — gley. Molluscs are generally present.
(4) Totally *aerobic sediments* — generally ploughwash — to the surface. Usually devoid of biological indicators.

In very large ditches, for example around towns or Roman forts, gradual infilling in the lower levels may lead to the formation of crude varves. This was the case in the main ditch of the Roman fort at Usk in South Wales where alternating bands of clay and sand were observed (W. H. Manning, pers. comm.).

Earthwork banks

In addition to the buried soil beneath an earthwork bank there are a few subsidiary sources of environmental data which can be obtained from within the bank itself.

Most commonly these are the secondary buried soils which form between two stages of earthwork construction (Fig.47). Iron Age hillforts, for example Danebury in Hampshire, often show two or more phases of enlargement, and the soil which forms between two such phases can yield information as to the land use of the site during its formation.

Secondly, where timber was used in the construction of a rampart, it was frequently burnt, and analysis of its charred remains yields evidence about contemporary tree species — although with the *caveat* that particular species may have been selected for rampart construction (p.25).

Thirdly, materials foreign to a site, such as river clays or turves brought from some distance, are sometimes incorporated, and molluscan, pollen and soil analysis can yield clues to their origin. For example, freshwater molluscs from terrestrial downland sites in north Wiltshire suggest the use of reed thatch or matting (Cunnington, 1931).

Pits, post-holes, wells and graves

There is a whole variety of features, other than ditches, that were constructed initially by excavation, and have later been subjected to infilling by natural and artificial processes. Few have been thoroughly investigated by the techniques of environmental archaeology. In dealing with these features the scientist considers three problems:

(1) The initial function.
(2) Any subsequent change of function.
(3) The general environment outside the feature.

Pits (Shackley, 1976). On the whole, pits on archaeological sites were used for storing grain or other food stuffs. They may subsequently have been used for disposing rubbish or for burial. Iron Age storage pits are often large, and if subsequent use has been minimal may show the same tripartite sequence seen in the larger ditches. Both molluscs and insects occur when conditions of preservation are suitable, the latter often giving detailed indication of the nature of the stored products.

At the Iron Age site of Danebury, Hampshire, fairly lengthy sequences of molluscan change have been preserved in the massive pits which are sometimes more than two metres deep. Although work at this site is in a preliminary stage, it can be said that information relating to both the later use of the pits and to the general environmental history of the site is being extracted. Similarly at Rams Hill in Berkshire, Bronze Age pit faunas were used convincingly to fill out the general picture of site history (Bradley and Ellison, 1975).

At the Butser experimental Iron Age farm in Hampshire, replicas of pits have been dug and filled with grain to test their suitability for storage (Reynolds, 1974). It is to be hoped that some of these when emptied will be allowed to fill up naturally so that the weathering processes in this sort of situation can be closely monitored and compared with the fill of Iron Age examples.

Cess pits are most commonly encountered on sites of historical age. They are often waterlogged, and in addition to the usual indicators, the remains of internal parasites of animals and man have been extracted in some cases (Pike and Biddle, 1966).

Post-holes. Post-holes are more difficult. They are often massive, as in the case of certain henge monuments — e.g. Durrington Walls in Wiltshire (Wainwright and Longworth, 1971) — but they present problems in that their fill is of such diverse origin (Fig.48). Thus the

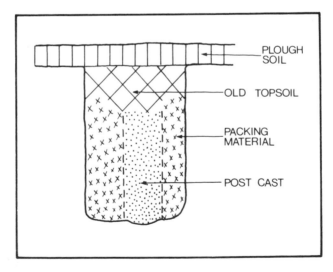

Fig.48. Section through a post-hole.

packing material around the post may contain topsoil contemporary with the digging of the post-hole, but it may not be possible
in the confined space between post-pipe and the geological solid to
determine the original orientation of this material. This is crucial
since soils are often closely stratified, and within a thickness of no
more than ten centimetres a number of different environments may
be represented. Then the *post-pipe* or *cast* may be infilled with
timber decayed *in situ*, or material that has fallen down the pipe
from above, or, if the post was removed, by part collapsed packing
and part topsoil. And finally, *subsidence* after the post has decayed
may incorporate soils and sediments formed initially on top of the
packing and post-pipe into lower levels.

Nevertheless, careful study may enable the separation and recog-
nition of these various sediments types, and the extraction of useful
environmental data. Practically nothing has yet been done.

A special type of post-hole situation is the *bedding trench* in
which a trench, rather than a hole, is dug for the setting of a row of
posts. The same difficulties apply but there is one added and
interesting complication. Post bedding trenches can be confused
with ice-wedge casts. This is not an academic problem, for mis-
identification has been made by both archaeologists and geologists
on a number of occasions (Evans, 1972b; Williams, 1973). Gravel
sites present the most difficulties. The main differences can be
enumerated as follows:

(1) In air view ice-wedge casts show a generally polygonal
pattern, although rectangular arrangements do occur. The
repeating reticulation is generally conclusive of a natural
origin (Fig.40).

(2) Again in air view, at the junction of two ice-wedge casts
there is a re-alignment towards the attainment of a right
angle if this is not the general relationship of the two casts in
the first place.

(3) On the ground there is no trace of individual post-pipes in
plan in an ice-wedge cast, and no charcoal or artefacts.

(4) In transverse section — which is where most confusion arises
— although there may be the semblance of a post-pipe in an
ice-wedge cast, the ambient subsoil is generally severely contorted in an upward or downward direction (Fig.41). Cutting
back into the subsoil provides the necessary proof.

Wells and shafts. The most useful information about the environment obtainable from wells and shafts is provided by waterlogged
material close to or at the base. A similar sequence of sediments to

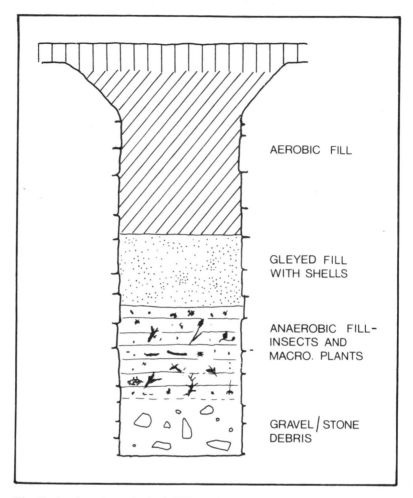

Fig.49. Section through the infilling of a well showing the various layers of sediment. Waterlogged ditches show a similar succession.

that in waterlogged ditches often occurs, and the same environmental indicators are applicable (Fig.49) (Evans, 1972a; Osborne, 1969; 1971).

Graves. Little environmental work has been done on graves. Where the subsoil is acid and the bones destroyed, their former presence can be verified by phosphate analysis or by the careful study of the grave fill in plan when a *stain* may be visible (Biek, 1969).

As with post-holes, the fill may be of diverse origin. Graves left open before backfilling may have a thin soil line close to the base which might be detectable by biological indicators.

On calcareous sites, two snail species are often common in grave and coffin fills — *Cecilioides acicula* and *Oxychilus cellarius*. Both are burrowing species, both like underground cavities, and *Oxychilus* is a carnivore. Neither can be used convincingly, however, to indicate whether a burial was made with flesh still preserved on the bones or whether the grave remained open or accessible for some time after the deposition of the burial as is occasionally claimed for Neolithic tombs. In Britain, *Cecilioides*, anyway, is an introduction of the medieval period.

Lynchets (Bowen, 1961; Fowler and Evans, 1967)

Lynchets are complex structures which represent the final stages of a series of processes. Essentially they are field boundaries which may be of various ages. Typically they are features of Lowland Zone Britain, appearing in downland areas as grassed-over terraces on hillsides (Fig.50). The initial stages of lynchet formation consist

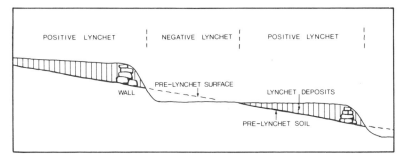

Fig.50. Transverse section through the lynchets of an ancient field system.

of the construction of a low bank or stone wall demarcating the field boundary and under which may be preserved a *buried soil*. Tillage, after the establishment of a field boundary, breaks up the soil and, if on a slope, hillwashing ensues. Soil builds up against the boundary on its uphill side resulting in the formation of a *positive* lynchet. Erosion on the downhill side creates a *negative* lynchet. After the fields are abandoned, deposition ceases and the lynchet and field surface become stabilized and grassed over.

Molluscan analysis has proved useful in studying lynchets of pre-historic and Romano-British age. Investigation of the buried soil will indicate whether or not there was a phase of cultivation prior to the establishment of the field boundary. The *lynchet deposits* may preserve buried soils indicative of standstill phases. Stripping of the soil inside the fields has sometimes revealed traces of cross-ploughing.

On the whole, the systems of small rectangular fields bounded by lynchets which are preserved on the downlands of southern Britain — the 'Celtic fields' — are of Iron Age date. Some systems continued in use into the Romano-British period but were eventually superseded by the open-field agriculture of Anglo-Saxon and medieval times, with its characteristic ridge-and-furrow ploughing.

However, recent work (Bowen, 1975) has shown that some Celtic fields are in fact of pre-Iron Age, probably Early/Middle Bronze Age, origin. Some occur in areas of downland that were later divided into much larger land units by *linear bank-and-ditch earthworks* known as 'ranch boundaries'. These are considered to be of late Bronze Age date. Where a ranch boundary crosses a lynchet there is high potential for environmental investigation from the following *loci* (Fig.51):

(1) Pre-lynchet soil.
(2) Lynchet deposits.
(3) Lynchet/ranch-boundary interface.

Furthermore, the lynchet and/or ranch boundary system may traverse dry valley deposits whose study can yield information about even earlier phases of land-use (Fig.51). Such potentially valuable sources of environmental evidence have barely begun to be tapped.

A similar system of linear stone banks, known as *reaves*, has been described from Dartmoor (Fleming, *et al.*, 1973) and these too are considered to be of late Bronze Age date. Pollen analysis of buried soils and adjacent peat deposits has been used to elucidate something of their environmental background.

Field walls

Although present under some lynchets, prehistoric and later field walls are most common in the Highland Zone of Britain (Feachem, 1973). Lynchets, by contrast, are less frequent. Field walls may be visible as surface systems, in which case they may be difficult to date unless tied into a settlement of known age. In recent years they

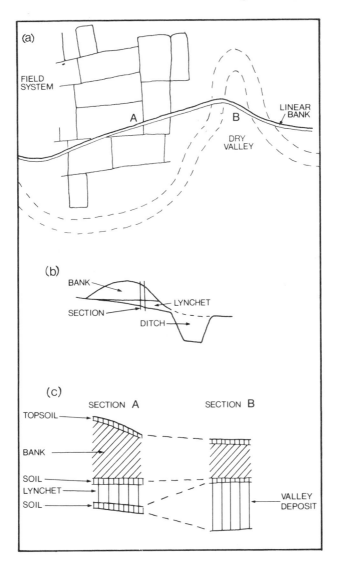

Fig.51. (a) Plan of a Bronze Age field system overlain by a linear earthwork ('ranch boundary') with the linear earthwork crossing a dry valley. (b) Skeleton section of the situation at point 'A' in (a). (c) Sections at 'A' and 'B' in (a) showing the relationship of the various deposits.

have been discovered under peat on a large scale — for example in Co. Mayo — and to a lesser extent under blown sand. In these cases there is a great potential for examining the pre-wall environment and, with regard to the possible reasons for the abandonment of the fields, the post-wall environment as well.

In addition to the field walls buried beneath blanket peat, traces of prehistoric field systems occur above the limits of later cultivation in areas where the soils are now podsolized. The two phenomena of peat formation and podsolization are the end results of soil degradation, but whether or not they were the cause of field abandonment or the result of it is not entirely clear (Limbrey, 1975). Climatic deterioration during the late-second and first millennia B.C., making cultivation of cereal crops at heights above about 300 metres practically impossible and enhancing the process of podsolization, was probably a contributory factor. But it is unlikely that soil degradation would have occurred had not man cleared the forest and tilled the soil in the first place.

In the Isles of Scilly there is a very impressive series of ancient field walls on the submerged flats between several of the islands. These are exposed at low tide.

Urban sites

The stratigraphy of urban sites is usually deep and complex. Buried soils, pits and ditches of various kinds, wells, thick occupation layers and graves may all occur juxtaposed, often intersecting. Cess pits are particularly common. A wider range of environmental evidence than usual is preserved in urban sites, especially water-logged deposits. This is partly because of the intensive occupation of the sites, resulting in a rapid buildup of occupation debris, and partly because of the rising water-table and flooding in the last 1,500 years or so — features exacerbated by the proximity of many towns to rivers.

A variety of environmental techniques needs to be applied. This has become realized in recent years with the growth of urban archaeology in the British Isles — York, Winchester, London, Viking Dublin — and an 'Environmental Archaeology Unit' has been established with success at York, where much prominence has been given to work on insect remains (Buckland, 1974). On the Continent and in European Russia, sites like Novgorod the Great (Thompson, 1967) have produced a whole succession of timber roadways which have enabled the establishment of a dendro-chronological sequence (Fig.12).

There are great opportunities in town sites for checking different kinds of environmental evidence against each other and for looking at contemporary evidence from different contexts, in this way getting a more balanced view of the overall environment. But the interpretation of the material is often tricky, in particular the distinction between climatic and local factors. For example, the temperature of towns today may be as much as five degrees centigrade higher than the surrounding rural areas, and the same may have been the case in the past. In this way, towns may have provided refugia for various species, particularly insects, well beyond their normal range.

Problems of contamination, particularly in large enclosed structures like sewers which do not become totally filled with sediment, are also severe (Buckland, 1976).

Tells

Tells are large, mostly artificial, settlement mounds which occur in the Balkans, Turkey, the Levant and east as far as Afghanistan. They may occupy areas of several hectares and be over fifteen metres high; e.g. Çatal Hüyük in Anatolia (Mellaart, 1967). Essentially they are ancient village or town sites formed by the successive construction, collapse/destruction, and replacement of houses made of mud-brick — the mud-brick being sun-dried river-derived silts and clays. This type of construction is only possible in areas with long hot dry summers, and is in marked contrast to the timber buildings of contemporary cultures in areas further to the north and west — most notably the long houses of Neolithic Europe. Many tells began their long history in early agricultural times — right at the beginning of the Post-glacial — and continued in use through into the historical period (e.g. French, 1973).

Several different loci could be sampled for environmental data. At the base of a tell (Fig.52) there is generally a buried land surface which may yield pollen, molluscan or pedological data about the pre-tell landscape. Phosphate and particle-size analysis of the tell sediments can give information about the rate of buildup and about breaks in continuity of occupation (Davidson, 1973). Molluscan analysis of the sediments, although never applied, would probably be of value as a source of information on the origin of the mud-brick and/or the nature of the riverine environment from which it was derived. Investigation — by the same techniques — of erosion products around the edge of the tell can yield something of its later environmental history and, if close to a river as many tells are, about the later history of the river — its sedimentation and lateral meanderings across the flood plain.

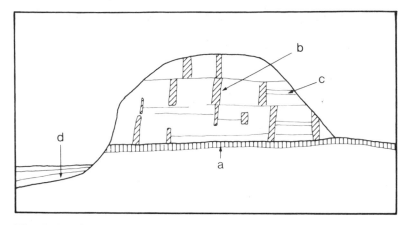

Fig.52. Vertical section through a tell. (a) pre-tell soil; (b) mud-brick walls; (c) tell material and occupation debris; (d) post-tell erosion deposits. All four loci can be used to provide environmental evidence.

Middens

Middens are artificial accumulations of human food debris and other wastes. The term 'midden' is usually applied to concentrations of this sort of material, particularly when occurring in the open as a visible mound. There is, however, no real difference in economic terms between this definition in the narrow sense and the occupation debris found outside caves, in hillfort ditches and on settlement sites. In some instances, traces of structures or huts may occur below, within or on top of a midden. On the whole these represent activity that occurred prior to, during standstill phases, or after midden accumulation, and are not contemporary with it. More generally, the midden and dwellings are adjacent but separate entities. A good example of this can be seen today on Samson, Isles of Scilly, where there are numerous eighteenth and nineteenth century cottages, now deserted and in ruins, each with its own shell midden a few metres away.

Middens preserve a whole variety of data of potential environmental value. Shellfish are usually common, but since they yield a far greater ratio of inedible material than any other animal, their importance in the economy may be overemphasized unless this fact is appreciated. In terms of their contribution to the human diet, mammals may be of equal or greater importance. Other groups often occurring in middens are fish and bird bones, Crustacea and sea urchin fragments. In exceptional cases organic material is preserved.

The study of middens is necessarily a study of the various animal and plant remains preserved in them, and on the whole lies in the field of economy. Coastal middens, such as those of the Danish Ertebølle Culture (Clark, 1975) or the thoroughly investigated site at Galatea Bay, New Zealand (Shawcross, 1967), are particularly suitable for study since their limits both temporally and spatially can often be clearly defined. *Total sampling/excavation* is only necessary if there is considerable lateral variation within a midden. Otherwise the midden can be divided by a grid of metre squares, and random squares then excavated. Large debris, such as shells and animal bone, can be extracted by the normal process of excavation, aided by a 0·5- or 1·0-cm mesh sieve. Everything should be recorded. Smaller material, especially fish bone, is best retrieved from *column samples* taken within each metre square excavated and sorted by fine sieving in the laboratory. In one comparative experiment thirty per cent more species of fish were found in this way (Casteel, 1976a). Flotation techniques can be applied for the recovery of plant debris and insect remains.

Although much of the debris from middens is of an economic kind it can still yield information of environmental value. For example:

(1) What habitats were being exploited by man in the food quest? Coastal, offshore, deep-sea, etc. And what animals?
(2) What was the relative importance of these various habitats and species? Were they all exploited at the same time?
(3) Was occupation seasonal or year-round, and if the former, at what season was the site occupied? (See p.62.)
(4) What was the size of the community using the midden?

In the environmental interpretation of midden material it is essential — as with all deposits of human food debris — to determine the extent to which the composition of the animal and plant assemblages in terms of species abundance is controlled by man — either directly by his hunting/gathering practices or indirectly by his affecting the habitat — and how far it is a reflection of the natural environment. This problem has already been discussed in the introduction to Chapter 3.

Another problem is the precise nature of the midden site. Sometimes middens may be separate mounds — discrete rubbish dumps — away from the main area of occupation. In other cases they may be intimately associated with occupation. In other cases they may be intimately associated with occupation structures, as in caves where layers are often rich in human coprolite. Ancient man was not always very fussy about separating the functions of eating and defaecation — as the high parasite content of some coprolites shows — and may even have carried on the two at precisely the same time on occasion. The distinction between the two types of midden is important in interpreting the environmental and economic significance of the biological remains. This applies particularly to organic material. For example, cereal grains from occupation contexts — storage pits, ovens or floors — are more likely to indicate the quality of the crop than those from a midden where the least valued parts of the diet are disposed (Dennell, 1976b).

The term midden is often used synonymously with *shell midden*. Although, as we have seen, a large variety of organic debris may occur in these sites, there is no doubt that they are especially frequent in coastal regions where they are indeed often made up largely of shell (Evans, 1969; Meighan, 1969). This phenomenon requires some explanation. Shell middens occur in many parts of the world. Some are coastal, such as those in western California, the Danish Ertebølle sites or the middens in Arnhem Land and Tasmania. Others occur inland along river banks, such as the Caspian middens of the Tagus in Portugal. Yet others occur along broad estuaries, notably the vast oyster mounds at Polmonthill and Inveravon on the south side of the Firth of Forth in Scotland. All this group are of peoples in the Mesolithic stage of development, peoples who were more or less entirely dependent on shellfish for all or part of the year. There has been much debate as to the reasons for this and the main hypotheses can be listed as follows:

(1) Post-glacial sea-level rise drove people from their favoured habitats on the rich grasslands of coastal areas to seek alternative food sources.

(2) Likewise, climate change at the end of the Ice Age necessitated a reorientation of food-getting strategies.

(3) The midden sites were occupied for only a part of the year, either when shellfish were particularly abundant, or while a coastal area was being exploited for other reasons; e.g. especially suitable raw materials.

(4) Post-glacial sea-level rise flooded earlier, Palaeolithic middens, resulting in a false concentration of sites in the Mesolithic time bracket.

(5) Shellfish are simply the normal diet for people living in the coastal zone.

The other main type of situation in which shell middens occur is on town sites, often well away from the coast. In this case, the shells are the remains of animals eaten not as a main component of the diet but as a delicacy.

There is no doubt that middens, in spite of the difficulties of their investigation, offer one of the best chances archaeologically of working out the total life-style and environment of early human communities.

Appendix

Chronological framework of main environmental and archaeological periods

The last two million years of earth history, constituting the Pleistocene Period, Quaternary or Great Ice Age, were characterized by strongly oscillating climatic conditions in which, during the cold oscillations, ice-sheets formed over Scandinavia, Britain and other parts of northern Europe as well as in North America. These cold stages are known as *glacials* or glaciations, the intervening warm stages as *interglacials*, and each is named after the site where it was first recognized. Unfortunately there is a profusion of schemes, but some of the more common are given in Table 3.

The main characteristics of a glacial period apart from the ice-sheets are (a) low sea-level caused by the locking up of water in the ice-sheets, (b) frost climates in areas where there are now temperate conditions, (c) various periglacial processes in areas peripheral to the ice-sheets, and (d) a characteristic fauna and vegetation.

Interglacials are characterized by a warming climate, high sea-levels, absence of strong physical weathering and a succession of vegetational changes leading ultimately to mixed deciduous woodland. There is a characteristic fauna.

The main zones of a typical glacial — interglacial — glacial sequence are indicated in Table 4.

The Late-Devensian and Flandrian periods have been particularly well studied and a number of zones, based on pollen analysis, have been recognized. These are indicated in Table 5 together with certain vegetational features, a more up-to-date zonation scheme, and the names given on the basis of late-nineteenth century peat bog studies.

In Tables 5 and 6 the positions of the main archaeological periods and some of their characteristics are indicated.

130

Table 3. Correlation of the main Pleistocene stages in various parts of the world. This is more intended as a guide to nomenclature rather than a statement of fact. Dates in millions of years before present.
w=warm stage (interglacial); c=cold stage (glacial).

	Britain	N. Europe	Alps	N. America	Others
w	Flandrian				Post-glacial, Holocene
	— 0·01				
c	Devensian	Weichselian	Würm	Wisconsin	Last Glaciation
	— 0·07				
w	Ipswichian	Eemian		Sangamon	Last Interglacial
c	Wolstonian	Saale	Riss	Illinoian	Penultimate Glaciation
w	Hoxnian	Holstein		Yarmouth	Penultimate, Great Interglacial
c	Anglian	Elster	Mindel	Kansan	Antepenultimate Glaciation
w	Cromerian	Cromerian		Aftonian	Antepenultimate Interglacial
	— 0·45				
	East Anglian Crags		Gunz	Nebraskan	Several alternate warm and cold stages
	— 2·0				
	Tertiary				

Table 4. The main zones of a glacial/interglacial succession in an area which today has a temperate climate. Interstadial periods of birch/pine woodland may occur in the early- and late-glacial zones (see Table 5).

Stage	Zone		Climate	Vegetation
Glacial	Early-glacial		Cold climate	Tundra/steppe
			Deteriorating	
Interglacial	IV	Post-temperate	Deteriorating climate	Pine/birch woodland
	III	Late-temperate		Increase of fir, and hornbeam
	II	Early-temperate	Climatic optimum	Mixed deciduous woodland
	I	Pre-temperate	Ameliorating climate	Birch/pine woodland
Glacial	Late-glacial		Cold climate	Tundra/steppe
			Ameliorating	
	Full-glacial		Ice sheets/ Arctic desert	Desert
	Early-glacial		Cold climate	Tundra/steppe
			Deteriorating	
Interglacial	IV	Post-temperate	Deteriorating climate	Pine/birch woodland

Table 5. Late-Devensian and Flandrian zonation schemes in Britain.

Recent zones and climate (Sparks and West, 1972)	Blytt and Sernander zones (p.23)	Pollen zones (p.16)	Vegetation	Archaeology (see Table 6)
Flandrian zone III	Sub-atlantic	VIII	Rise of ash, birch, beech and hornbeam	Historical
	Sub-boreal	VIIb		
Decreasing warmth				Iron Age
			Increase of open land	Bronze Age
			Elm decline	Neolithic
Flandrian zone II	Atlantic	VIIa	Mixed oak forest plus alder	
Climatic optimum				
Flandrian zone I	Boreal	VI	Mixed oak forest plus hazel and pine	Mesolithic
Increasing warmth		V		
	Pre-boreal	IV	Birch and pine	
Late-Devensian zones				
III Cold	Younger Dryas	III	Tundra	Upper
II Amelioration (see p.48)	Allerød	II	Birch woods	Palaeolithic
I Cold	Older Dryas	I	Tundra	

Table 6. The main archaeological periods in the British Isles. Dates back to 8300 B.C. either historical or based on varve or dendrochronological correction of radiocarbon determinations (pp.28 and 30); dates prior to 8300 B.C. in millions of years before present, and based on radiocarbon and potassium-argon (p.110).

Historical period	Roman, Dark Age, Medieval, Post-medieval.
— A.D. 43	
Iron Age	Use of Iron for tools and weapons.
— 650 B.C.	
Bronze Age	Use of Bronze for tools and weapons.
— 2500 B.C.	
Neolithic — 4500 B.C.	New Stone Age. Introduction of farming, pottery and ground stone axes.
Mesolithic — 8300 B.C.	Hunting and food-gathering communities living in Post-glacial forest environments.
Upper Palaeolithic — 0·03	Hunting communities living in Ice Age steppe and tundra environments. First true modern man, *Homo sapiens sapiens*.
Middle Palaeolithic — 0·1	Hunting communities living in the later part of the Pleistocene. Neanderthal Man, *Homo sapiens neanderthalensis*.
Lower Palaeolithic	Hunting and food-gathering communities living in a variety of environments — cold and warm, open and forest — from the Late Tertiary onwards. Early forms of man, e.g. *Australopithecus* (not known from Britain).

Glossary of terms not formally explained in the text

Acid. Relating to soils of pH less than 7·0, which are sour, poor in nutrients and support an impoverished vegetation, e.g. of heath. Or relating to rocks with a high silica (SiO_2) content and which give rise to acid soils. Chemically *an acid* is a compound with hydrogen in an ionic — or reactive — state, which is corrosive and which neutralizes alkaline substances.

Aerobic. Relating to situations in which oxygen is present and in which microbial decay takes place.

Algae. A group of lower plants which includes microscopic unicellular forms like diatoms and larger forms such as seaweeds.

Alkaline (or basic). Relating to soils of pH above 7·0, which are generally rich in nutrients and have a high calcium content. Or relating to rocks poor in silica (cf. *acid*).

Anaerobic. Relating to situations in which oxygen is lacking and in which microbial decay does not take place.

Anthropogenic. Relating to man.

Augering. Use of a boring tool with a screw-point for bringing up samples of sediment.

Australopithecine. Relating to *Australopithecus*, an early form of man or ape-man occurring mainly in Africa.

Barrows. Bronze Age and Neolithic (sometimes later) burial mounds consisting of a heap of earth and rock, and surrounded by a ditch or ditches. Neolithic barrows are long or round, Bronze Age barrows always round.

Basic. See *alkaline*.

Bronze Age. The prehistoric period succeeding the Neolithic which saw the introduction of bronze for tools and weapons (Table 6).

Calcareous. Relating to the chemical compound calcium carbonate ($CaCO_3$) of which chalk and limestone are largely composed. Or referring to soils with a high calcium carbonate content and which are alkaline.

Calcium carbonate. See *calcareous*.

Carbon dioxide. A gas, present in the atmosphere in the concentration of 0·03% (chemical formula CO_2). Dissolves in water to form the weak acid *carbonic acid* (H_2CO_3).

Carr. A type of woody vegetation consisting of trees like hazel, alder and willow which develops on very peaty soils, generally in lowlying situations (p.107).

135

Causewayed camp. A type of Neolithic monument occurring in southern Britain, consisting of a circular enclosure demarcated by a bank and ditch with many causeways.

Chlorides. See *halides*; also p.105.

Decachiliad. A period of 10,000 years.

Ecology. The study of animals and plants in relation to their environment.

Environment. The total surroundings of an organism — all factors that in any way affect its mode of life.

Flint mine. A shaft, sometimes over 12 metres deep, typically of Neolithic Age, occurring in chalk areas and dug for the extraction of flint for making axes and other tools.

Fossil. Relating to an organism, archaeological feature or a landscape no longer living or functioning, and which has been preserved. Technically the term fossil refers to an organism whose chemical composition has been altered after death or which is preserved only as a cast or trace. (Cf. *subfossil*.)

Habitat. The place where an animal or plant lives — its immediate surroundings.

Halides. Mineral salts of chlorine and iodine. Common rock salt (NaCl) is a halide.

Hand-axe. Characteristic tool of Lower Palaeolithic man, consisting of a large core of flint or other stone worked to a point at one end and a butt at the other. It was probably held in the hand and used as an all-purpose tool for clubbing, skinning, piercing, etc.

Henge. A type of late Neolithic or early Bronze Age ceremonial monument consisting of a circular bank and ditch. There is usually one or more entrance.

Hillfort. An Iron Age or later Bronze Age fortification consisting of an area defended by massive banks and ditches.

Hillwash. Soil accumulation in valley bottoms (p.70).

Hydrogen peroxide. A chemical (H_2O_2) which breaks down soil crumbs. Also used as a bleaching agent, e.g. for hair.

Igneous rocks. Rocks formed by volcanic activity (e.g. basalt, obsidian) or by the subsurface upwelling of molten masses (e.g. granite).

Interglacial. A period of temperate climate between two cold or glacial stages (Table 4).

Interstadial. A period of mild climate, within a generally cold or glacial stage, in which birch or pine (but not mixed deciduous) woodland may develop.

Iodides. See halides; also p.105.

Iron Age. The period of prehistory which was characterized by the use of iron for tools and weapons (Table 6).

Iron oxides. Compounds of iron (chemical formula e.g. Fe_2O_3), oxygen and sometimes water molecules which have a red, brown or yellow colour. They constitute the basis for pigments like red and yellow ochre, and are an important component in soil.

Isotope. A variety of a chemical element. Isotopes of the same element — e.g. of carbon (C) — have different physical properties, particularly weight, but identical chemical properties. There are three isotopes of carbon, C-12, C-13 and C-14, the number referring to the atomic weight relative to that of the hydrogen atom which is one. Some isotopes are radioactive — i.e. they change to other elements or isotopes at a known rate, emitting sub-atomic particles in the process.

Long barrows. See *barrow.*

Lower Palaeolithic. Relating to that part of the Old Stone Age prior to the evolution of modern man, *Homo sapiens sapiens.*

Mass spectrometer. Machine for measuring the atomic weight (mass) of an element and hence for distinguishing between different elements and different isotopes of the same element.

Mesolithic. Relating to the period in prehistory immediately following the Ice Age but before the development of farming, when people still lived by hunting and food-gathering.

Mould-board plough. A type of plough fitted with a wooden board at an angle just behind the share which was capable of turning the soil right over. Probably present in Britain by late Roman times and certainly during the Anglo-Saxon period. Associated with ridge-and-furrow cultivation.

Neanderthal. Relating to a type of man, *Homo sapiens neanderthalensis,* living between about 100,000 and 30,000 years ago, and characterized by features such as heavy bone structure, receding forehead, prominent brow ridges, and receding lower jaw.

Neolithic. Relating to the New Stone Age or period of prehistoric farming prior to the introduction of metal-working (Table 6).

Neutral. Relating to soils which are neither acid nor alkaline; pH 7·0.

Obsidian. A black volcanic glass.

Palaeoecology. The study of ancient animals and plants in relation to their environment.

Palaeolithic. (=Old Stone Age). Relating to Stone Age peoples living by hunting and food-gathering without the knowledge of farming or the use of metals. In north-west Europe the term is applied to the period prior to the Flandrian.

Periglacial. Relating to the zone around an ice-sheet where frost-weathering processes take place (p.95).

Permafrost. Permanently frozen ground. A characteristic feature of many parts of Ice Age Europe and North America which now enjoy a temperate climate. Permafrost obtains today in the extreme north of North America and Siberia.

Phylum. A category of animal or plant classification lesser than a 'kingdom', including species obviously related to each other but not to species in other phyla. Typical phyla are the Protozoa (single-celled animals), Annelida (worms) and Echinodermata (starfish, sea-urchins, etc.).

Radiocarbon dating. A method of dating organic material — timber, bone, peat, etc. — by assaying the radioactive isotope C-14 (Renfrew, 1973). The technique can be used back to 70,000 years ago. See also p.30 and Fig.13.

Refugia. Small isolated areas inhabited by an animal or plant species outside the main distribution of that species.

Ridge-and-furrow cultivation. A method of ploughing land with a mould-board plough in long strips which results in the formation of ridges often up to five metres wide. Characteristic of Anglo-Saxon and medieval farming. Ridge cultivation is much older, but the width of the ridges is less and they may have been produced by spade.

Ring cairn. Bronze Age burial monument consisting of a ring — rather than the normal mound — of piled stones, enclosing an area in which burials were placed.

Round barrow. See *barrow*.

Sarsen. A type of siliceous rock which occurs on parts of the chalkland plateau of southern England, generally as individual rocks. Some of these may weigh several tons, and the larger ones were used in the construction of prehistoric stone circles, e.g. Stonehenge.

Scanning electron microscope. A type of electron microscope which enables surface textures of objects to be examined, and which produces a 3-D image.

Silica. A chemical compound, oxide of silicon (SiO_2), of which quartz, flint and glass are largely composed.

Siliceous. Relating to silica.

Subfossil. Relating to a dead and preserved organism whose chemical composition has not been altered from that in life.

Tectonic. Relating to the up and down movement of the earth's crust.

Tertiary. The geological period prior to the Quaternary, extending back 70 million years or more.

Upper Palaeolithic. Relating to that part of the Old Stone Age equivalent to the emergence of modern man, *Homo sapiens sapiens*. Lasted from approximately 35,000 to 10,000 years ago (Table 6).

Vector. A carrier, or transmitter, of a disease or parasite. The snail, *Lymnaea truncatula*, is the vector of the liver fluke or sheep.

Bibliography

The following are recommended as introductory and non-technical works:

Clark, J. G. D. 1952. *Prehistoric Europe: The Economic Basis.* Methuen, London.
Cornwall, I. W. 1964. *The World of Ancient Man.* Phoenix House, London.
Dimbleby, G. W. 1967. *Plants and Archaeology.* John Baker, London.
Dimbleby, G. W. 1977. *Ecology and Archaeology.* Edward Arnold, London.
Evans, J. G. 1975. *The Environment of Early Man in the British Isles.* Paul Elek, London.
Mitchell, F. 1976. *The Irish Landscape.* Collins, London.
Sparks, B. W. and West, R. G. 1972. *The Ice Age in Britain.* Methuen, London.

More advanced compilations are:

Butzer, K. W. 1972. *Environment and Archaeology.* Methuen, London.
Brothwell, D. and Higgs, E. S. (Eds.), 1969. *Science in Archaeology.* Thames and Hudson, London.
Davidson, D. A. and Shackley, M. L. (Eds.), 1976. *Geoarchaeology: Earth Science and the Past.* Duckworth, London.
Evans, J. G. and Limbrey, S. (Eds.), 1975. *The Effect of Man on the Landscape: the Highland Zone.* Council for British Archaeology, London.
Godwin, H. 1956. *The History of the British Flora.* Cambridge University Press, London.
West, R. G. 1968. *Pleistocene Geology and Biology with Especial Reference to the British Isles,* Longman, London.

References cited in the text

The following abbreviations have been used:
J. Arch. Sci. — *Journal of Archaeological Science*
Phil. Trans. — *Philosophical Transactions of the Royal Society*
P.P.S. — *Proceedings of the Prehistoric Society*
Otherwise, abbreviations are those given in the *World List of Scientific Periodicals* and the *Biosis List of Serials*.

Ager, D. V. 1963. *Principles of Palaeoecology*. McGraw-Hill, New York.

Allison, M. J., Pezzia, A., Hasegawa, I. and Gerszten, E. 1974. 'A case of hookworm infestation in a pre-Columbian American.' *Am. J. phys. Anthrop.* **41**, 103-6.

Atkinson, R. J. C. 1957. 'Worms and weathering.' *Antiquity* **31**, 219-33.

Bannister, B. 1969. 'Dendrochronology.' *In* D. Brothwell and E. S. Higgs (Eds.), *Science in Archaeology*. Thames and Hudson, London, 191-205.

Benson, D. G. and Miles, D. 1974. *The Upper Thames Valley: An Archaeological Survey of the River Gravels*. Oxfordshire Archaeological Unit, Oxford.

Biek, L. 1969. Soil silhouettes. *In* D. Brothwell and E. S. Higgs (Eds.), *Science in Archaeology*. Thames and Hudson, London, 118-23.

Birks, H. H. 1975. Studies in the vegetational history of Scotland IV. Pine stumps in Scottish blanket peats. *Phil. Trans.* B **270**, 181-226.

Bishop, M. J. 1974. Preliminary report on the Middle Pleistocene mammal bearing deposits of Westbury-sub-Mendip, Somerset. *Proc. speleol. Soc.* **13**, 301-18.

Blytt, A. 1876. *Essay on the Immigration of the Norwegian Flora during Alternating Rainy and Dry Periods*. Cammermeyer, Christiania.

Bonny, A. P. 1972. A method for determining absolute pollen frequencies in lake sediments. *New Phytol.* **71**, 393-405.

Bowen, D. Q. 1973. The excavation at Minchin Hole 1973. *Gower* **24**, 12-18.

Bowen, H. C. 1961. *Ancient Fields*. British Association, London.

Bowen, H. C. 1975. Air photography and the development of the landscape in central parts of southern England. *In* D. R. Wilson (Ed.), *Aerial Reconnaissance for Archaeology*. Council for British Archaeology, London, 103-18.

Bradley, R. and Ellison, A. 1975. *A Bronze Age Defended Enclosure and its Landscape*. British Archaeological Reports, Oxford.

Brothwell, D. 1972. *Digging up Bones*. British Museum, London.

Brothwell, D. and Brothwell, P. 1969. *Food in Antiquity*. Thames and Hudson, London.

Buchsbaum, R. 1951. *Animals without Backbones*. Penguin, Harmondsworth.

Buckland, P. C. 1974. Archaeology and environment in York. *J. Arch. Sci.* **1**, 303-16.

Buckland, P. C. 1976. *The Environmental Evidence from the Church Street Roman Sewer System.* Council for British Archaeology, London.

Buckland, P. C., Greig, J. R. A. and Kenward, H. K. 1974. York, an early medieval site. *Antiquity* **48**, 25-33.

Butzer, K. W. 1972. *Environment and Archaeology.* Methuen, London.

Callen, E.O. 1969. Diet as revealed by coprolites. *In* D. Brothwell and E. S. Higgs (Eds.), *Science in Archaeology.* Thames and Hudson, London, 235-43.

Case, H. 1969. Settlement-patterns in the north Irish Neolithic. *Ulster Journal of Archaeology* **32**, 3-27.

Casteel, R. W. 1976a. Comparison of column and whole unit samples for recovering fish remains. *World Archaeology* **8**, 192-6.

Casteel, R. W. 1976b. *Fish Remains in Archaeology and Paleo-environmental Studies.* Academic Press, London.

Chaplin, R. E. 1971. *The Study of Animal Bones from Archaeological Sites.* Seminar Press, London.

Clark, J. G. D. 1952. *Prehistoric Europe: The Economic Basis.* Methuen, London.

Clark, J. G. D. 1954. *Excavations at Star Carr.* Cambridge University Press, London.

Clark, J. G. D. 1967. *The Stone Age Hunters.* Thames and Hudson, London.

Clark, J. G. D. 1975. *The Earlier Stone Age Settlement of Scandinavia.* Cambridge University Press, London.

Coles, J. M., Hibbert, F. A. and Orme, B. J. 1973. Prehistoric roads and tracks in Somerset: 3. The Sweet track. *P.P.S.* **39**, 256-93.

Coles, J. M., Orme, B. J., Hibbert, F. A. and Jones, R. A. 1975. *Somerset Levels Papers: No. 1.* Department of Archaeology, University of Cambridge.

Coope, G. R. 1967. The value of Quaternary insect faunas in the interpretation of ancient ecology and climate. *In* E. J. Cushing and H. E. Wright (Eds.), *Quaternary Palaeoecology.* Yale University Press, New Haven and London, 359-80.

Coope, G. R. and Angus, R. B. 1975. An ecological study of a temperate interlude in the middle of the Last Glaciation, based on fossil Coleoptera from Isleworth, Middlesex. *J. Anim. Ecol.* **44**, 365-91.

Coope, G. R. and Brophy, J. A. 1972. Late-glacial environmental changes indicated by a coleopteran succession from North Wales. *Boreas* **1**, 97-142.

Coope, G. R., Shotton, F. W. and Strachan, I. 1961. A Late Pleistocene fauna and flora from Upton Warren, Worcestershire. *Phil. Trans.* B **244**, 379-421.

Cornwall, I. W. 1953. Soil science and archaeology with illustrations from some British Bronze Age monuments. *P.P.S.* **19**, 129-47.

Cornwall, I. W. 1956. *Bones for the Archaeologist.* Phoenix House, London.

Cornwall, I. W. 1958. *Soils for the Archaeologist.* Phoenix House, London.

Cornwall, I. W. 1964. *The World of Ancient Man.* Phoenix House, London.

Cornwall, I. W. 1968. *Prehistoric Animals and their Hunters.* Faber and Faber, London.

Crampton, C. B. and Webley, D. P. 1964. Preliminary studies of the historic succession of plants and soils on selected archaeological sites in South Wales. *Bulletin of the Board of Celtic Studies* **20**, 440-9.

Cunnington, M. E. 1931. The 'Sanctuary' on Overton Hill, near Avebury. *Wilts. archaeol. nat. Hist. Mag.* **45**, 300-35.

Darwin, C. 1881. *The Formation of Vegetable Mould through the Action of Worms with Observations on their Habitats.* Murray, London (Republished in 1945 by Faber and Faber as *Darwin on Humus and the Earthworm* with an introduction by Sir Albert Howard.)

Davidson, D. A. 1973. Particle size and phosphate analysis — evidence for the evolution of a tell. *Archaeometry* **15**, 143-52.

Dawson, E. W. 1969. Bird remains in archaeology. *In* D. Brothwell and E. S. Higgs (Eds.), *Science in Archaeology.* Thames and Hudson, London, 359-75.

Degerbøl, M. and Krog, H. 1951. Den europaeiske Sumpskildpadde (*Emys orbicularis* L.) i Danmark. *Danm. geol. Unders.* II Rk. Nr. 78.

Dennell, R. W. 1976a. Prehistoric crop cultivation in southern England. *Antiquaries Journal* **56**, 11-23.

Dennell, R. W. 1976b. The economic importance of plant resources represented on archaeological sites. *J. Arch. Sci.* **3**, 229-47.

Denton, G. H. and Karlén, W. 1973. Holocene climatic variations — their pattern and possible cause. *Quaternary Research* **3**, 155-205.

Dickson, J. H. 1973. *Bryophytes of the Pleistocene.* Cambridge University Press, London.

Dimbleby, G. W. 1961. Soil pollen analysis. *J. Soil Sci.* **12**, 1-11.

Dimbleby, G. W. 1962. *The Development of the British Heathlands and their Soils.* Oxford Forestry Memoir No. 23, Oxford.

Dimbleby, G. W. 1967. *Plants and Archaeology.* John Baker, London.

Dimbleby, G. W. 1976. Review of J. G. Evans 1975, *The Environment of Early Man in the British Isles.* Paul Elek, London. *Antiquity* **50**, 81-2.

Dimbleby, G. W. and Evans, J. G. 1974. Pollen and land-snail analysis of calcareous soils. *J. Arch. Sci.* **1**, 117-33.

Dimbleby, G. W. and Speight, M. C. D. 1969. Buried soils. *Advmt Sci., Lond.* **26**, 203-5.

Elton, C. 1927. *Animal Ecology.* Sidgwick and Jackson, London. (Republished in 1966 by Methuen.)

Evans, J. G. 1969. The exploitation of molluscs. *In* P. J. Ucko and G. W. Dimbleby (Eds.), *The Domestication and Exploitation of Plants and Animals.* Duckworth, London, 477-84.

Evans, J. G. 1972a. *Land Snails in Archaeology.* Seminar Press, London.

Evans, J. G. 1972b. Ice-wedge casts at Broome Heath, Norfolk. *P.P.S.* **38**, 77-86.

Evans, J. G. 1975. *The Environment of Early Man in the British Isles.* Paul Elek, London.

Evans, J. G. and Limbrey, S. (Eds.) 1975. *The Effect of Man on the Landscape: the Highland Zone.* Council for British Archaeology, London.

Evens, E. D., Grinsell, L. V., Piggott, S. and Wallis, F. S. 1962. Fourth report of the sub-committee of the south-western group of museums and art galleries on the petrological identification of stone axes. *P.P.S.* **28**, 209-66.

Faegri, K. and Iversen, J. 1964. *Textbook of Pollen Analysis.* Blackwell, Oxford.

Feachem, R. W. 1973. Ancient agriculture in the highland of Britain. *P.P.S.* **39**, 332-53.

Fleming, A. and Collis, J. with Jones, R. L. 1973. A late prehistoric reave system near Cholwich Town, Dartmoor. *Proceedings of the Devon Archaeological Society* No. 31, 1-21.

Fowler, P. J. and Evans, J. G. 1967. Plough-marks, lynchets and early fields. *Antiquity* **41**, 289-301.

French, D. 1973. Aşvan 1968-1972: an interim report. *Anatolian Studies* **23**, 71-307.

Frey, D. G. 1964. Remains of animals in Quaternary lake and bog sediments and their interpretation. *Arch. Hydrobiol. Beih.* **2**, 1-114.

Funnell, B. M. 1961. The Paleogene and Early Pleistocene of Norfolk. *Trans. Norfolk Norwich Nat. Soc.* **19**, 340-64.

Funnell, B. M. and West, R. G. 1962. The Early Pleistocene of Easton Bavents, Suffolk. *Q. Jl geol. Soc. Lond.* **118**, 125-41.

van Geel, B. 1976. Fossil spores of Zygnemataceae in ditches of a prehistoric settlement in Hoogkarspel (the Netherlands). *Rev. Palaeobot. Palynol.* **22**, 337-44.

Glob, P. V. 1969. *The Bog People: Iron-Age Man Preserved.* Faber and Faber, London.

Godwin, H. 1940. A Boreal transgression of the sea in Swansea Bay. *New Phytol.* **39**, 308-21.

Godwin, H. 1944. Age and origin of the 'Breckland' heaths of East Anglia. *Nature* **154**, 6.

Godwin, H. 1956. *The History of the British Flora.* Cambridge University Press, London.

Godwin, H. and Tansley, A. G. 1941. Prehistoric charcoals as evidence of former vegetation, soil and climate. *J. Ecol.* **29**, 117-26.

Gresswell, R. K. 1957. *The Physical Geography of Beaches and Coastlines.* Hutton, London.

Gresswell, R. K. 1958a. *The Physical Geography of Rivers and Valleys.* Hutton, London.

Gresswell, R. K. 1958b. *The Physical Geography of Glaciers and Glaciation.* Hutton, London.

Hallam, B. R., Warren, S. E. and Renfrew, C. 1976. Obsidian in the western Mediterranean: characterization by neutron activation analysis and optical emission spectroscopy. *P.P.S.* **42**, 85-110.

Heizer, R. F. 1969. The anthropology of prehistoric Great Basin human coprolites. *In* D. Brothwell and E. S. Higgs (Eds.), *Science in Archaeology*. Thames and Hudson, London, 244-50.

Helbaek, H. 1952. Early crops in southern England. *P.P.S.* **18**, 194-230.

Helbaek, H. 1969. Palaeo-ethnobotany. *In* D. Brothwell and E. S. Higgs (Eds.), *Science in Archaeology*. Thames and Hudson, London, 206-14.

Higgs, E. S. and Vita-Finzi, C. 1972. Prehistoric economies: a territorial approach. *In* E. S. Higgs (Ed.), *Papers in Economic Prehistory*. Cambridge University Press, London, 27-36.

Higham, C. F. W. 1969. Towards an economic prehistory of Europe. *Curr. Anthropol.* **10**, 139-50.

Hole, F. and Flannery, K. V. 1967. The prehistory of southern Iran: a preliminary report. *P.P.S.* **33**, 147-206.

Iversen, J. 1941. Landnam i Danmarks Stenalder. *Danm. Geol. Unders.* II Rk. Nr. 66, 1-68.

Jarman, H. N., Legge, A. J. and Charles, J. A. 1972. Retrieval of plant remains from archaeological sites by froth flotation. *In* E. S. Higgs (Ed.), *Papers in Economic Prehistory*. Cambridge University Press, London, 39-48.

Jarman, M. R. 1972. European deer economies and the advent of the Neolithic. *In* E. S. Higgs (Ed.), *Papers in Economic Prehistory*. Cambridge University Press, London, 125-49.

Jelgersma, S. 1966. Sea-level changes during the last 10,000 years. *In* J. S. Sawyer (Ed.), *World Climate from 8000 to 0 B.C.* Royal Meteorological Society, London, 54-71.

Jewell, P. A. and Dimbleby, G. W. 1966. The Experimental Earthwork on Overton Down, Wiltshire, England: the first four years. *P.P.S.* **32**, 313-42.

John, B. S. 1970. Pembrokeshire. *In* C. A. Lewis (Ed.), *The Glaciations of Wales and Adjoining Regions*. Longman, London, 229-65.

Kelly, M. R. 1964. The Middle Pleistocene of North Birmingham. *Phil. Trans.* B **247**, 533-92.

Kerney, M. P. 1963. Late-glacial deposits on the Chalk of south-east England. *Phil. Trans.* B **246**, 203-54.

Kerney, M. P. 1971. Interglacial deposits in Barnfield Pit, Swanscombe, and their molluscan fauna. *J. Geol. Soc.* **127**, 69-93.

Kerney, M. P., Brown, E. H. and Chandler, T. J. 1964. The Late-glacial and Post-glacial history of the Chalk escarpment near Brook, Kent. *Phil. Trans.* B **248**, 135-204.

Klein, R. G. 1975. The ecology of Stone Age man at the southern tip of Africa. *Archaeology* **28**, 238-47.

Klima, B., Kukla, J., Ložek, V. and de Vries, H. 1962. Stratigraphie des Pleistozäns und alter des Paläeolithischen Rastplatzes in der Ziegelei von Dolní Vestonice (unter-Wisternitz). *Anthropozoikum* **11**, 93-145.

Kubiëna, W. L. 1953. *The Soils of Europe*. Thomas Murby, London.

Kurtén, B. 1968. *Pleistocene Mammals of Europe*. Weidenfeld and Nicolson, London.

Lamb, H. H. 1972. *The Changing Climate*. Methuen, London.

Limbrey, S. 1975. *Soil Science and Archaeology.* Academic Press, London.

Ložek, V. 1964. Quartärmollusken der Tschechoslowakei. *Rozpr. ústřed. Úst. geol.* **31**, 1-374.

Ložek, V. 1967. Climatic zones of Czechoslovakia during the Quaternary. *In* E. J. Cushing and H. E. Wright (Eds.), *Quaternary Paleoecology.* Yale University Press, Newhaven and London, 381-92.

Lumley, H. de 1972. *La Grotte de l'Hortus.* Centre National de la Recherche Scientifique, Marseille.

Mackereth, F. J. H. 1966. Some chemical observations on Post-glacial lake sediments. *Phil. Trans.* B **250**, 165-213.

Mania, D. 1973. Paläoökologie, Faunenentwicklung und Stratigraphie des Eiszeitalters im mittleren Elbe-Saalegebiet auf Grund von Molluskengesellschaften. *Geologie* **21**, 1-175.

Manley, G. 1962. *Climate of the British Scene.* Collins. London.

Megard, R.O. 1967. Late Quaternary Cladocera of Lake Zeribar, western Iran. *Ecology* **48**, 179-89.

Meighan, C. W. 1969. Molluscs as food remains in archaeological sites. *In* D. Brothwell and E. S. Higgs (Eds.), *Science in Archaeology.* Thames and Hudson, London, 415-22.

Mellaart, J. 1967. *Çatal Hüyük. A Neolithic Town in Anatolia.* Thames and Hudson, London.

Mitchell, F. 1976. *The Irish Landscape.* Collins, London.

Norton, P. E. P. 1967. Marine molluscan assemblages in the Early Pleistocene of Sidestrand, Bramerton and the Royal Society borehole at Ludham, Norfolk. *Phil. Trans.* B **253**, 161-200.

Odum, E. P. 1963. *Ecology.* Holt, Rinehart and Winston, New York.

Osborne, P. J. 1969. An insect fauna of Late Bronze Age date from Wilsford, Wiltshire. *J. Anim. Ecol.* **38**, 555-66.

Osborne, P. J. 1971. An insect fauna from the Roman site at Alchester, Warwickshire. *Britannia* **2**, 156-65.

Osborne, P. J. 1976. Evidence from the insects of climatic variation during the Flandrian period: a preliminary note. *World Archaeology* **8**, 150-8.

Pennington, W. 1943. Lake sediments: the bottom deposits of the north basin of Windermere, with special reference to the diatom succession. *New Phytol.* **42**, 1-27.

Pennington, W. 1970. Vegetation history in the north-west of England: a regional synthesis. *In* D. Walker and R. G. West (Eds.), *Studies in the Vegetational History of the British Isles.* Cambridge University Press, London, 41-79.

Pike, A. W. and Biddle, M. 1966. Parasitic eggs in medieval Winchester. *Antiquity* **40**, 293-6.

Pitty, A. F. 1971. *Introduction to Geomorphology.* Methuen, London.

Proudfoot, B. 1976. The analysis and interpretation of soil phosphorus in archaeological contexts. *In* D. A. Davidson and M. L. Shackley (Eds.), *Geoarchaeology: Earth Science and the Past.* Duckworth, London, 116-35.

Raikes, R. 1967. *Water, Weather and Prehistory.* John Baker, London.

Read, H. H. 1962. *Rutley's Elements of Mineralogy*. George, Allen and Unwin, London.

Renfrew, C. 1973. *Before Civilisation: The Radiocarbon Revolution and Prehistoric Europe*. Jonathan Cape, London.

Reynolds, P. J. 1974. Experimental Iron Age storage pits: an interim report. *P.P.S.* **40**, 118-31.

Rosenfeld, A. 1965. *The Inorganic Raw Materials of Antiquity*. Weidenfeld and Nicolson, London.

Rosholt, J. N., Emiliani, C., Geiss, J., Koczy, F. F. and Wangersky, P. J. 1961. Absolute dating of deep-sea cores by the Pa^{231}/Th^{230} method. *J. Geol.* **69**, 162-85.

Russell, E. J. 1961. *The World of the Soil*. Collins, London.

Russell, F. S. and Yonge, C. M. 1936. *The Seas*. Warne, London.

Ryder, M. L. 1969. Remains of fishes and other aquatic animals. *In* D. Brothwell and E. S. Higgs (Eds.), *Science in Archaeology*. Thames and Hudson, London, 376-94.

Sampson, C. G. 1974. *The Stone Age Archaeology of Southern Africa*. Academic Press, London.

Schmid, E. 1969. Cave sediments and prehistory. *In* D. Brothwell and E. S. Higgs (Eds.), *Science in Archaeology*. Thames and Hudson, London, 151-66.

Schove, D. J. and Lowther, A. W. G. 1957. Tree rings and medieval archaeology. *Medieval Archaeology* **1**, 78-95.

Schultz, C. B. and Martin, L. D. 1970. Quaternary mammalian sequences in the Central Great Plains. *In* W. Dort and J. K. Jones (Eds.), *Pleistocene and Recent Environments of the Central Great Plains*. Kansas University Press, Kansas, 341-53.

Seaward, M. R. D. and Williams, D. 1976. An interpretation of mosses found in recent archaeological excavations. *J. Arch. Sci.* **3**, 173-7.

Seddon, B. 1962. Late-glacial deposits at Llyn Dwythwch and Nant Ffrancon, Caernarvonshire. *Phil. Trans.* B **244**, 459-81.

Sernander, R. 1908. On the evidence of Post-glacial changes of climate furnished by the peat mosses of northern Europe. *Geol. För. Stockh. Förh.* **30**, 465-78.

Shackleton, N. J. 1969a. Marine Mollusca in archaeology. *In* D. Brothwell and E. S. Higgs (Eds.), *Science in Archaeology*. Thames and Hudson, London, 407-14.

Shackleton, N. J. 1969b. The last interglacial in the marine and terrestrial records. *Proc. R. Soc.* B **174**, 135-54.

Shackleton, N. J. 1973. Oxygen isotope analysis as a means of determining season of occupation of prehistoric midden sites. *Archaeometry* **15**, 133-41.

Shackley, M. L. 1975. *Archaeological Sediments: A Survey of Analytical Methods*. Butterworths, London.

Shackley, M. L. 1976. The Danebury project: an experiment in site sediment recording. *In* D. A. Davidson and M. L. Shackley (Eds.), *Geoarchaeology: Earth Science and the Past*. Duckworth, London, 9-21.

Shawcross, W. 1967. An investigation of prehistoric diet and economy on a coastal site at Galatea Bay, New Zealand. *P.P.S.* **33**, 107-31.

Shotton, F. W. 1968. Prehistoric man's use of stone in Britain. *Proc. Geol. Ass.* **79**, 477-91.

Smith, A. G. 1970. The influence of Mesolithic and Neolithic man on British vegetation: a discussion. *In* D. Walker and R. G. West (Eds.), *Studies in the Vegetational History of the British Isles.* Cambridge University Press, London, 81-96.

Smith, A. G. and Pilcher, J. R. 1973. Radiocarbon dates and vegetational history of the British Isles. *New Phytol.* **72**, 903-14.

Sparks, B. W. 1957. The non-marine Mollusca of the interglacial deposits at Bobbitshole, Ipswich. *Phil. Trans.* B **241**, 33-44.

Sparks, B. W. 1961. The ecological interpretation of Quaternary non-marine Mollusca. *Proc. Linn. Soc. Lond.* **172**, 71-80.

Sparks, B. W. 1969. Non-marine Mollusca and archaeology. *In* D. Brothwell and E. S. Higg (Eds.), *Science in Archaeology.* Thames and Hudson, London, 395-406.

Sparks, B. W. 1971. *Rocks and Relief.* Longman, London.

Sparks, B. W. and Lambert, C. A. 1961. The Post-glacial deposits at Apethorpe, Northamptonshire. *Proc. Malac. Soc.* **34**, 302-15.

Sparks, B. W. and West, R. G. 1972. *The Ice Age in Britain.* Methuen, London.

Spencer, P. J. 1975. Habitat change in coastal sand-dune areas: the molluscan evidence. *In* J. G. Evans and S. Limbrey (Eds.), *The Effect of Man on the Landscape: the Highland Zone.* Council for British Archaeology, London, 96-103.

Stuart, A. J. 1976. The history of the mammal fauna during the Ipswichian/Last Interglacial in England. *Phil. Trans.* B **276**, 221-50.

Tankard, A. J. and Schweitzer, F. R. 1976. Textural analysis of cave sediments: Die Kelders, Cape Province, South Africa. *In* D. A. Davidson and M. L. Shackley (Eds.), *Geoarchaeology: Earth Science and the Past.* Duckworth, London, 289-316.

Tansley, A. G. 1939. *The British Isles and their Vegetation.* Cambridge University Press, London.

Tauber, H. 1967. Differential pollen dispersion and filtration. *In* E. J. Cushing and H. E. Wright (Eds.), *Quaternary Palaeoecology.* Yale University Press, New Haven and London, 131-41.

Taylor, E. L. 1955. Parasitic helminths in mediaeval remains. *The Veterinary Record* **67**, 216-18.

Thomas, W. L. (Ed.) 1956. *Man's Role in Changing the Face of the Earth.* Chicago University Press, Chicago.

Thompson, M. W. 1967. *Novgorod the Great: Excavations at the Medieval City 1951-62 by A. V. Artsikhovsky and B. A. Kolchin.* Evelyn, Adams and Mackay, London.

Tringham, R. 1971. *Hunters, Fishers and Farmers of Eastern Europe: 6000-3000 B.C.* Hutchinson, London.

Turner, J. 1965. A contribution to the history of forest clearance. *Proc. R. Soc.* B **161**, 343-53.

Turner, J. 1975. The evidence for land use by prehistoric farming communities: the use of three-dimensional pollen diagrams. *In* J. G. Evans and S. Limbrey (Eds.), *The Effect of Man on the Landscape: the Highland Zone*. Council for British Archaeology, London, 86-95.

Ucko, P. J. and Dimbleby, G. W. (Eds.) 1969. *The Domestication and Exploitation of Plants and Animals*. Duckworth, London.

Ucko, P. J. and Rosenfeld, A. 1967. *Palaeolithic Cave Art*. Weidenfeld and Nicolson, London.

Vereshchagin, N. K. 1975. The mammoth from the Shandrin River. *Vestnik Zoologii*, **2**, 81-4.

Vita-Finzi, C. 1969. *The Mediterranean Valleys*. Cambridge University Press, London.

Waateringe, W. G.-van 1968. The elm decline and the first appearance of *Plantago maior*. *Vegetatio* **15**, 292-6.

Wainwright, G. J. and Longworth, I. H. 1971. *Durrington Walls: Excavations 1966-1968*. Society of Antiquaries, London.

Walker, D. 1955. Skelsmergh Tarn and Kentmere, Westmorland. *New Phytol*. **54**, 222-54.

Watling, R. and Seaward, M. R. D. 1976. Some observations on puffballs from British archaeological sites. *J. Arch. Sci*. **3**, 165-72.

Webley, D. 1974. An early record of *Heterodera humuli* Filipjev in the United Kingdom. *Nematologica* **20**, 262.

Wells, C. 1964. *Bones, Bodies and Disease*. Thames and Hudson, London.

West, R. G. 1961. Vegetational history of the Early Pleistocene of the Royal Society borehole at Ludham, Norfolk. *Proc. R. Soc*. B **155**, 437-53.

West, R. G. 1968. *Pleistocene Geology and Biology with especial reference to the British Isles*. Longman, London.

Williams, D. 1976. A Neolithic moss flora from Silbury Hill, Wiltshire. *J. Arch. Sci*. **3**, 267-70.

Williams, J. Ll. and Jenkins, D. A. 1976. The use of petrographic, heavy mineral and arc spectrographic techniques in assessing the provenance of sediments used in ceramics. *In* D. A. Davidson and M. L. Shackley (Eds.), *Geoarchaeology: Earth Science and the Past*. Duckworth, London, 116-35.

Williams, R. G. B. 1973. Frost and the works of Man. *Antiquity* **47**, 19-31.

Wymer, J. 1968. *Lower Palaeolithic Archaeology in Britain*. John Baker, London.

Zeuner, F. E. 1959. *The Pleistocene Period: Its Climate, Chronology and Faunal Successions*. Hutchinson, London.

Zeuner, F. E. 1963. *A History of Domesticated Animals*. Hutchinson, London.

Index

149